A
Soldier's
Armageddon

A
Soldier's
Armageddon

by
James B. Simms

Sunflower University Press®

1531 Yuma • P. O. Box 1009 • Manhattan, Kansas 66505-1009 USA

Cover from *The Epic of the 101st Airborne — A Pictorial Record of a Great Fighting Team*, 101st Airborne Division Public Relations Office, Auxerre, France, 1945.

Edited by Carole Chelz

Layout by Lori L. Daniel

ISBN 0-89745-227-5

Sunflower University Press is a wholly-owned subsidiary of the non-profit 501(c)3 Journal of the West, Inc.

Civilization is a game of inches that never ends. This book is dedicated to Capaletti, my partner who fell in combat, . . . and to every man, woman, and child who has fallen in the advancement or preservation of the principles of civilized behavior. They were not cold statistics in a history book. They were human beings who were terribly afraid but who were anchored by their bravery and commitment.

And to my wife Dot, and my two children, whose patience made this work possible.

.

Contents

Preface

SOME 20 YEARS AFTER the end of World War II, I became aware that many books had been written and movies made about generals, admirals, battles, tactics, politicians, and nations, but not much about the personal life of the U.S. wartime serviceman who disappeared overseas to surface again sometime later in one of four different forms: intact but changed, broken in mind, broken physically, or in a box.

War is the method man devised in order to mass produce bitter grief, unbearable suffering, and total misery; but fight wars we must. For every noble humanitarian that is born there are 100 would-be Hitlers, and when a Hitler comes along we either have to pay the price of the installment on civilization or we can default and bankrupt civilization into the dark age, which is worse than war. Sometimes, in war there is hope.

I began this effort in the late 1960s but almost gave up because getting it typed, edited, and retyped was causing problems. Also, during the war in Vietnam, half the country was doing the wrong thing for the right reasons and the other half was doing the right thing for the wrong reasons. Everyone was pursuing his own prejudices until I didn't think that anyone would be interested in the lives and efforts of the serviceman, who mainly was just following orders as decreed by the President and Congress.

In the 1980s I mentioned this book to Allan LeBaron, a retired U.S. Navy sailor, and he not only insisted that I finish it but typed the whole thing on his computer to facilitate the editing.

In April 1945, a 12-year-old Belgian boy, without any prompting, had told me the way the Cold War would develop. Remembering his account now is almost like recalling a history that has been forgotten by a whole generation. The irony of this particular part of the book is that I finished my work at the very time the Berlin Wall was coming down.

James B. "Dude" Simms

Introduction

I WAS BORN DECEMBER 21, 1918, 40 days after the Armistice of World War I. My generation would be the one that fought World War II.

My generation is unique in the history of mankind because in one hand we held the westward-moving pioneer and in the other the astronaut. If in 1925, when I was six years old, you could have suddenly transported me back to 1825, I would have been in more familiar surroundings than if you had transported me forward to 1985. My Grandpa Burgess was born in 1849, and Grandma Burgess was born in 1852. Grandma Simms was born during the Civil War. The many things related to me about these times of long ago made the history and literature of the 19th century more alive and interesting because I had heard so many first-hand accounts about the era.

Grandma Burgess told me about the time during the Civil War when she and her Mother were washing clothes at a spring and some soldiers came by. While the soldiers were eating, and drinking from the spring, they began to laugh and joke and compare their souvenirs, which were human ears and human fingers. I don't think my grandmother was impressed, so let me tell you something. If you want to impress a girl or a woman, don't show her your gore, show her your mind, and for a condiment sprinkle on a tiny bit of your soul. It works "purty" good.

Three things stand out to me while I was growing up that seem almost universal to my generation. First, ours was the last age where most of the children helped the family make a living, either on the farm, in the family store, repair shop, coal yard, or in 101 other ways. Second, in my generation it was almost universal that each family ate its meals together around the family table — the best family bond and character-building thing that one can do. Little ears hear all sorts of things that promote manners and attitude.

I know when I was very small I found out that Mama would not let us eat out of a common bowl with our personal fork or spoon. She said to do so would make the food very unappetizing to some people — my first lesson about other people's feelings. She also knew in those days before refrigerators that to seed the germs of the mouth into warm food would speed up the spoilage.

And third, my generation was the last one where parents developed an uncanny judgment as to when to apply "the rod." We did not consider this abuse because we were about half mule and there was some kind of a deep understanding about "tough love." It was a happy badge of status in school to be able to claim parents who gave the hardest whipping. There was no resentment.

My generation became the big sisters and big brothers to the children of the world because we truly had a way with children. If you don't believe me, just ask "Kilroy," that ever-present "traveler" of World War II, known to every serviceman. Kilroy was everywhere — seemed to be aware of everything! If you don't believe Kilroy, look at the statistics and see how many babies were born just after World War II.

Chapter One

Heroes and Personalities

*T*HE PURPOSE OF THIS BOOK is to observe some of the things pertinent to human nature in order that we might better understand just what makes us tick. By following the soldier's life in combat, after combat, and back to civilian life, the observations and meanings of this experience become clear. Some of the personalities that I observed in men in combat are distinct enough to use as models.

First there are the heroes. I have picked three of these as fairly typical of the type: the Reluctant Hero, the Naive Hero, and the Fearless Foster. The Reluctant Hero is usually a rather well-balanced and mature type who knows how to get along with people. He may be an extrovert, but not necessarily, and in general he doesn't care too much for extremely high intellectual pursuits. If this man is young, he is a well-balanced sort for his age. He is well aware of the dangers and his chances. He is not interested in being a hero, but in staying alive and doing his job. Usually this type is somewhat individualistic in nature and is not very much concerned with the spit and polish of ceremony. If he is confronted with the situation where it is only he who can save the group, he will quickly exhaust the various alternatives, if any, and will then approach the task of knocking out an enemy position with all the judgment he possesses. He will go about the task using the safest and surest method available to him and if successful will be fully aware of — but stunned by — the enormity of his success.

The Naive Hero is apt to be young, and, if not young, more likely to be of the indoor or clerical type rather than the aggressive outdoor type. He always performs his duties well, always passes inspection, is neat and quiet and is usually well-liked, although his choice of free-time activities may not be the same as that of his fellow soldiers. He will be more apt to go sightseeing, take photographs, or go to the movies, while the Reluctant Hero more likely will be participating in less strenuous activities, like barroom brawling.

If the Naive Hero is confronted with the burden of saving his group, he is not as likely to consider alternatives, but might immediately rush headlong into his task. If he succeeds, he is not so aware of the enormity of his deed but most usually will be aware that he is scared to hell and gone! Quite a few of this kind get picked off early in their combat career; but if they survive to gain experience and judgment, they are apt to become top-flight combat men.

The third type of hero, the Fearless Foster, is self-confident and, if intelligent, nearly always knows his job. Danger does not affect old Fearless as it does the average person; it seems to thrill and stimulate him, and he is at his best when the going gets rough. If Fearless Foster is confronted with a situation that lays the burden on him to save the group, he might well haughtily stride forward (no bullet would have the audacity to strike him) and the last thing the enemy would see would be his withering look of contempt. Fearless takes to leadership like a duck to water, and most often he has compassion for men not so brave and leans enough to thoughtful considerations so as not to be too reckless. He is the dream of the Army War College.

Personalities in combat also fall into several other categories, and although they usually are more complex than can be described by a single characterization, they do have some traits that stand out. The first type is what I call the Shell, or the imitator. This man does not have deep inner strength. Instead, through the years he has built around himself an outer covering that presents an appearance resembling Fearless Foster, but there is a lot of space between this outer shell and his inner strength. He is an imitator because he tries to imitate his ideal, Fearless Foster; but unfortunately, they are made of different stuff. When the Shell is exposed to his first great baptism of fire, he is vulnerable to cracking up at once — a catastrophic blow to his ego, because lesser men are sticking it out while he is reduced to a blubbering coward.

Another type is what I call the Scared Rabbit, though ironically sometimes I think that of all the combat men he is the only one who has good sense. Scared Rabbit obeys the laws of instinct. If he runs into anything that he can't handle, he simply believes in going the other way. Some people might get him confused with the Shell, but he is a different breed. If you tell a joke that has a really sharp point, he'll *miss* the point. If he tells a joke, it won't have a point. The Shell may crack up; the Scared Rabbit usually doesn't. His heart is in the right place; it's "foot trouble" he has. To state it simply, he is not emotionally complex. He has a simple philosophy: when the going gets rough, get the hell out of there.

Another personality is what I call the Low Key type. Low Key is likely to be comparatively easy-going. He probably is a victim of circumstance as much as anything else. He is basically a pretty honest fellow, and he may range from fairly low to very strong inner strength. I would think that the stronger his inner resolve, the more catastrophic his cracking up would be. He doesn't usually crack in his first battle, although he suffers greatly. Later, after an interval of calm or rest during which he worries about future engagements, he runs out of will power as things begin to get hot again. He doesn't try to fake or hide anything, he just simply tells the medics that he has "had it" and cannot go on. He is a pretty good fellow if the pressure doesn't get too great.

Also in combat is the Bitter End. Bitter End is a fine fellow. He resembles and is related to both the Reluctant Hero and the Naive Hero; he does not give up easily. He is dedicated to doing his part, and when he reaches the point of no return, he refuses to quit. Consequently, he will stick it out till the "bitter end." When Bitter End finally cracks, he usually loses contact with reality — whereas when Low Key cracks, he usually retains this contact.

The Indefinite is another personality of combat. His problem may come in several different ways, and his trouble is not the problem, but the way he tries to solve it. He may "bug out" to a safer place when the going gets tough, or he may try to play sick, or pretend to be in another place. If he were always perfectly frank, he would be much better off than to try to conceal his intentions and his actions. His ego will not allow him to admit defeat, yet he will connive to try to stay alive. I call him Indefinite because he may be a real soldier today and evasive tomorrow, or vice versa.

Chapter Two

Airborne Humor and Joining the 101st Airborne

*I*N THE FIRST HALF OF November 1944, I joined the U.S. Army's 101st Airborne Division near Rheims, France, at a small place called Mourmelon-le-Grand. My basic training was in Combat Intelligence and Reconnaissance, after which I went through the Parachute Jump School and then the Parachute Riggers School. I learned to pack and repair every kind of parachute made, plus aerial delivery practice and techniques. When I was finally assigned to the 101st Airborne, I was attached to the anti-tank platoon, Headquarters Company, 1st Battalion, 506th Parachute Infantry. This suited me fine. I was home at last.

While I was taking paratroop training at Fort Benning, Georgia, an incident occurred that still amuses me. We were over the worst of our physical training, all the "weak sisters" had fallen by the wayside, and those remaining were a bunch of hard-headed knuckleheads who would almost jump from a plane without a parachute if the instructor had given the word. One morning we fell out in formation. It was hot as the devil and we were hoping that we would have it a little easier that day. A very correct and tough First Lieutenant was in charge of the Training Company. He clicked his heels together (he was already slough footed), pumped himself up like a big frog, and bellowed "Compa-*nay!*" In the split-second pause before the Lieutenant bellowed out "Ten-*chut*," a perfect Donald Duck voice from the rear ranks squeaked, "Platoon, Ten-*chut.*" As the Lieutenant was finishing his order, the whole company burst out laughing. The Lieutenant turned red in the face and related what he thought of a company that would laugh while at "Attention." And to reinforce this little lecture we were ordered to do 50 pushups. Pushups were standard punishment in the paratroop school, and the rule was that who gives mass punishment has to do it also.

So we did 50 pushups, and then the Lieutenant said he guessed that would teach us a lesson. He clicked his heels again, pumped himself up, and then bellowed "Comp-*nay!*"

The duck voice responded again with, "Who does that SOB think he is?" And as the Lieutenant boomed out his "Ten-*chut!*" the company once again burst out laughing.

The Lieutenant was fit to be tied. He didn't know what we were laughing about and he didn't appreciate it a bit. So we did 50 more pushups, and by then sweat was really pouring. After another gnarly lecture, he clicked his heels and got himself all swelled up as he fairly screamed "Compa-*nay!*"

The duck spoke again: "The old boy's face is getting red." When the thundering "Ten-*chut!*" descended, the company burst out laughing, again. The whole situation was becoming ridiculous, and I was expecting the Lieutenant to start going for his hair any moment.

This confusing situation went on until we had been given 200 pushups. Finally, some of the men close to this duck character told him that if he didn't stop his morbid recreation he would be taken care of — but good. I shared a pup tent in England with this nut, and I'm still chuckling.

We had many interesting and funny incidents in training, typical of the happy-go-lucky, go-to-hell attitude of the airborne troops.

James B. Simms.

When we had arrived at the main camp of the 101st Airborne Division in France, we were immediately divided into groups, assigned to our respective units, and the Captain gave us a wise little talk. He told us that the veterans in the outfit were combat-weary and were pretty tough hombres. We were not to expect them to rush out and welcome us with open arms; they would need a little time to look us over. The wise thing for us to do, he noted, was to keep our mouths shut and our eyes and ears open. If we would do this, we would be accepted right into the family. I found this to be very good advice.

I had stayed in a rear echelon camp in England for a short time, and I had already seen that there was a difference in the combat veteran *vs*. the new recruit. I had noticed that the horseplay of the veterans sometimes approached mayhem. I remember one night a bunch in the next Quonset hut were amusing themselves by pitching handfuls of M1 ammo into the stove, just to watch it blow the lid off. When they tired of this innocent little game, they began placing quarter-pound blocks of TNT under the corner of their hut and detonating them. The officer of the guard, tiring of this juvenile approach to recreation, put the whole hut under house arrest, placed guards at the door, and wouldn't even let the men go out to the latrine.

Shortly after I was assigned, I was attracted to one man by his friendly attitude and by his accent, which I recognized as being from my part of the country. Vernon Agy hailed from Memphis, Tennessee, less than 200 miles from my home. I became accepted by my new outfit through our football team. I had played a little college ball, so I went out for the 506th Regimental team and was soon playing fullback. If the weather was okay, we did a little light military training in the morning and we practiced football in the afternoon — though most often in the rain.

For evening recreation, we had USO shows every few nights. When there was not a show we would huddle around in the cold unheated barracks and "shoot the bull." A day room had been made from an old barn or stable, and occasionally it would be open and would have good kraut beer for sale at ten cents per canteen cup. The room would also have an open barrel half full of glowing coals — coke — and this warmth was most welcome.

One day, we moved from our barracks to a building just across the street. It was of typical masonry construction and had only one door, midway in the barracks. Inside, there was a small room at one end to which I was assigned, which could accommodate about three double-decker bunks. In the main room, the double-decked bunks were placed end-to-end around the entire floor space, leaving only a small passageway to the door.

One particularly dark gloomy night, the day room was open and no USO shows were scheduled, so I went in, had a couple of canteen cups of good beer, warmed myself by the coke barrel, and had a very enjoyable time. When I went to bed back at the barracks, I promptly fell asleep. After an hour or two, however, that beer began to try to make bond. I awakened, thought "No sweat, I'll just slip on my pants and boots and step outside to the latrine." I didn't put on my shirt, and that is where I made my mistake, because my matches were in my shirt pocket. The lights were out and even outside it was as dark as a stack of black cats at midnight. In addition, the barracks was fitted with very effective black-out curtains and was in a state of total darkness. You couldn't see a mess kit placed directly in front of your eyes.

I left my bunk in this small end room and felt for the door that led to the main room. When I touched a smooth wall, I knew I had missed the door. I thought I would go back to my bunk and start over, but when I couldn't find any bunk or the wall I realized that I had gone into the big room, and I didn't know which way to go to reach the outside door. I decided to try going back to the little room door and begin again, and promptly ran into someone's bunk, clanging the mess kit hanging on the corner post. Every way I turned, I would run into a mess kit. I realized that I was hopelessly lost in my own barracks.

Total darkness does funny things to you. Because you can't see anything to give you perspective, it affects your balance. After banging into several bunks, I finally sank down and from a sitting position tried to contemplate my fate. If this had happened later, after I had become adjusted to my new friends, I would have bellowed for someone to strike a match; but at the stage I was in, I was reluctant to tell anyone that I was hopelessly lost in my *own* barracks. I finally decided that my only hope was to crawl on my hands and knees until I hit a bunk, then crawl along hitting the bunks, until I found the passageway to the door. The whole thing would have amused me, except that a little voice inside my bladder was beginning to scream that time was growing short. It seemed as if I crawled all the way around the barracks before I found the door to get outside. I have never been more *relieved*!

As the new men became more adjusted to the outfit, they were able to talk more freely with the combat veterans. I heard Vernon Agy say several times that if we caught another mission he might have to shoot himself in the leg before he would go back into combat, but I don't think any of the men who knew him believed that.

The unofficial scuttlebutt had it that our next mission would be to jump the Rhine River in the upcoming all-out Spring offensive.

Chapter Three

Bastogne, Belgium

*A*BOUT TWO O'CLOCK ON A Sunday or Monday morning, I was rudely shaken by a soldier who told everyone to get up and start packing — we had another mission! The urgency at this time of night struck a chill into me, for I knew it could not be a jump, because we had not been supplied, organized, or briefed. I didn't know that the terrible Battle of the Bulge had begun.

As we began packing our surplus items in duffel bags to be left behind, and getting dressed in the clothes we would wear into battle, I noticed that before most men were half packed Agy was ready and waiting. During the day we were issued ammo, K-rations, and other available supplies that we might need. We were advised to wear plenty of clothing, and I had on winter underwear, two pair of pants, two shirts, two field jackets, and an overcoat. Added to this were a pack, two bandoliers of M1 ammo, my M1, and 25 pounds of bazooka ammo. I looked like a fat duck trying to waddle.

Early that afternoon we fell out, and the Captain gave us a short briefing to let us know what type of people we were going to be running up against. He told us about the Malmédy Massacre where German SS troops had killed large numbers of surrendered American prisoners. The Malmédy Massacre of December 17, 1944, has been widely depicted as having occurred in the snow; it did not snow at Bastogne, Belgium, however, where we were, until we had been there two or three days, and we knew about Malmédy before we left base. Whether there could have been that much difference in the climate between Bastogne and Malmédy I don't know, though the U.S. Army *Official Histories* show a scene of dead men in the snow at Malmédy.

About four o'clock on the afternoon of the new mission we crowded into big Army transport trucks (semi-trailers) and rode until early dawn the next morning. It was an unbearably miserable night with men and weapons in a hopeless tangle, trying to rest when rest was impossible. We arrived and unloaded on the outskirts of Bastogne just before the light of dawn. We bivouacked temporarily in a grove of evergreens. As I lay on my blanket and tried to get some sleep in that cold misty weather, apprehension was beginning to build and little did I realize what I was really in for.

My assignment was as ammunition bearer to a young man named Cappaletti. He had been in combat before and that automatically made him the gunner on the bazooka. This seemed right, because the ammo was a lot heavier than the bazooka, and I was bigger than he. We had been in the grove only about an hour, when we were given the order to prepare to move out. We were told to leave anything we didn't need in a pile, and soldiers began to drop any excess baggage they didn't want to carry. If I had known how long our march would be that day I would have left my coat, but I was green and was unaware of all these things about combat.

As we began to move out, our Regimental Commander, Colonel Robert Sink, was watching us go by. We called him "Uncle Bob" or "Colonel Bob," and he was a pistol if there ever was one. As we filed past, we were dressed in everything except uniformity, and it gave a very ragged-looking appearance. "Uncle Bob" said to a soldier just ahead of me, "Where is your overcoat?"

"It's back in the pile, sir."

Colonel Sink snorted. "I'll be damned if this don't look like one ragged ass army!"

I thought I caught something in his attitude that was more than met the eye. I don't think he cared a bit how we looked; this was just his way of charging everyone up for the task that was ahead, and he was more aware of this than were we.

As we set out on this long forced march that would take us to battle, there was a lot of thinking I had to do. I was a little apprehensive about the man I had been teamed with. Cappaletti was obviously of Italian extraction, probably from a big northern city. I was Anglo-Saxon Scotch-Irish from the rural South. Boys reared on a farm are notorious for their distrust of city-bred boys when it comes to sharing hard physical labor. I just barely knew the guy by sight, and had no idea whether he would be careless, reckless, or have any other quirks that might not add to our well-being. As it turned out, I need not have worried because we went through our combat together without one cross word. He was as willing to work and dig as I, and he was neither reckless nor careless. We thought so much alike that we did things without even having to discuss the proper way.

We marched along on our way to battle, and there were a great many other concerns I had to deal with. When we reached combat, would I throw down my rifle and run? Would I be reduced to a blubbering coward, or would I be able to keep my head up, my nerves calm and stand all the fear and adversities? Many men think they know themselves, but none can be sure of their reaction or behavior until they come up against the rock. Not even heroes know that they will have courage until the circumstance that triggers their reaction has occurred. Some facet of our personalities are moved into behaving one way or another in extreme conditions.

We could hear artillery booming in the distance, as we walked along the road, and in various directions. I thought it sounded just like a big training base; but this was no training, this was for real. To realize that people are out there with the complete dedication and intention of killing you is a sobering and disquieting thought — a physical enemy, a real presence, a person trained to annihilate you.

We walked for miles, and the farther we went the more my gear and my clothes became a burden. By noon I was sweating like it was the middle of July, and yet the temperature was in the high 30s. Finally I became so hot that I knew I must get rid of my overcoat. I transferred my ammo pack to my right arm, then I removed my pack with my left hand and held it with my right arm. I took the two bandoliers of M1 ammo from around my neck and shoulders and placed them on my right arm. At this point I was holding on my right shoulder, arm, and hand an M1 rifle, 25 pounds of bazooka ammo, my rifle ammo, and my pack. I slung and jerked until I got my left arm out of my overcoat sleeve, then I transferred all this equipment to my left arm and shucked off the overcoat. I pitched it to the side of the road and proceeded to put my equipment back in place. All this took place while marching at forced march pace and without losing my position in line. I must have looked very strange indeed! Finally we came off the secondary road and went onto the main highway between Bastogne and Noville, at a little village called Foy. We didn't know the names of these places ahead of time, but we were to become very familiar with them in the future.

About halfway between Foy and Noville we came to a most welcome stop. We had been marching for hours, and with all those clothes and equipment I was really suffering. As we stood there for a short time I heard a hair-raising sound and, immediately, the Belgian man who was acting as our guide jumped behind the road embankment. When he jumped, I jumped, and about a second later this wild banshee screaming sound passed overhead and landed somewhere to our rear. I had heard my first "screaming meemies" — the German shells so-named originally in World War I, which we called "rockets" — and no one had to tell me what they were. Their sound was self-explanatory.

By that time I was beginning to be filled with deep anxiety and apprehension because it was apparent that we were getting close to what we had come for. A tank sitting in the edge of the field down toward Noville had been hit and knocked out. The men in the tank scrambled out and began running across the field in the general direction of Bastogne. The anxiety this produced in a "green" soldier just before battle is a distressing thing; he doesn't know what to expect, how to act, or how he will react.

After a while, we began moving again and soon we came to a rise in the highway where we could look down on Noville about 400 or 500 yards away. We stopped on this rise and after standing there for a moment one of our Lieutenants said, rather matter-of-factly, "They are going to throw in a little artillery, after which we are going to move through this little town." He added, "I don't think there will be anything much down there." That was the extent of our briefing for what lay ahead.

The American Army has a "thing" about artillery. I believe if the Army only had one cannon and one shell it would feel compelled to fire before an attack to make damn sure that the enemy would know we were coming. Artillery in massive quantities concentrated in small areas can be an awesome and destructive weapon, but a few rounds thrown in to precede an attack is of little tactical value. If I were a commander and my artillery was limited, I would begin the attack and when the enemy had to expose himself to shoot back, that is when I think a limited amount of artillery would be most effective. But then I'm not a commander.

As we waited on this rise overlooking Noville, my anxiety level tightened up like a banjo string. A Lieutenant, who was nervously pacing back and forth, said to a soldier standing with his head and shoulders out of a tank destroyer, "Man, this is going to be a bastard." The man in the tank destroyer readily agreed. This didn't have any soothing effect on my nerves, and to add to it, the soldier in the tank noticed that I didn't have an entrenching tool of any kind.

"Hey, Mac," he called, "I see you don't have a shovel. Here, you can have mine." I politely declined, and he said, "Hell, you better take it, you're going to need it worse than I am."

I took the shovel and hung it on my belt. For more than just this one instance, I came to respect the boys in the tank destroyers. We had three or four TDs to support us when we went to Noville that afternoon, and that was all the armor we had that I knew about. But then there were things going on of which I was unaware.

Presently the artillery that had been screaming over our heads seemed to slacken, and at this instant, as if someone had pushed a master button, all hell broke loose. To someone who has never been in the middle of a vicious fire fight, there is no adequate way to explain it. The movies simply cannot duplicate it. The din of the roaring, buzzing sound was deafening as countless automatic weapons spoke in unison. When you're in the center of a fire fight such as this you can't distinguish the individual burst of the machine guns. When you're some distance away from a big fire fight, many individual bursts can be heard.

As this unbelievable fire power began, the adrenaline hit me. I had been an athlete, had gone through jump training, and had been in some sticky positions before, so I was acquainted with this adrenaline business, but you've never had it kick in so fast until you suddenly get that baptism in battle. My legs were so weak that water would seem to be a rock-hard solid if I walked on it. It is a good thing that we crouched down at this instant because I would surely have fallen down. Bullets began to ricochet through the limbs of an apple tree that stood on the edge of the highway, a mortar shell burst just off the road, and, to me, things were looking bad. Cappaletti was crouched down intently peering down the highway toward Noville. I didn't know how to act, except to try not to look scared; but all the time my insides were churning around like a washing machine. Fear that hits a green combat man before he learns to handle it is enough to turn his brains to jelly.

We had already loaded the bazooka and all I knew what to do was to just follow Cap wherever he went — that is, if my legs would support me. Cap had never tried to give me any instructions or orders as is sometimes the case with an egotistical gunner, so when he suddenly rose and started running toward Noville, he never said a word or looked back. I can only suppose that somehow he knew I would be with him, so there was no need to tell me.

We ran about half the distance and hit the ground just off the highway against the embankment. A medic was treating a serious wound on a soldier nearby, and in my state of mind you can imagine how unpleasant all that blood looked. After we got our wind a bit, Cap jumped up and started running again. With all the lead flying around I don't know how we hadn't already been hit, but we were still going.

Noville was a long, narrow town. It was built straddling the highway, like many small towns in Europe, about a quarter-mile in length from end to end. As we approached the first building we saw two jeeps that had been knocked out. They were very close together, facing each other at about a 30-degree angle. Cap raced around the jeeps, but to gain a little advantage in time I went between them. Since they were so close together, I placed my left hand on one of the hoods and jumped over the bumpers of both. As I sailed to the other side, there suddenly appeared before me a sickening sight. On the pavement, were two men that I recognized as having shipped overseas with my group. One was face down, but the kid I knew best was open-eyed and staring straight at me. Both were dead. I don't believe in levitation, but somehow I changed direction in midair and landed on the other side of the boy and kept running.

As we ran up the main street of Noville, Cap would suddenly stop and flatten himself in a doorway and I would do the same. By the time we made it to the other end of town, the firing seemed to be slowing down a bit and we encountered our Platoon Lieutenant and Sergeant. Sergeant Morris told us that we needed to go with him. He was trying to round up enough men to make up a patrol to go and establish contact with another company. That suited me all right because I didn't know where I was going, where I had been, or even where I was, so for someone to tell me exactly what to do was welcome. It is unbelievable how confused a novice can be in his first big battle.

On our way to the other end of Noville I was aware of many things that were happening, but most of them didn't seem to have any sense or reason.

Cap filled me in on one thing. There seemed to have been a kraut sniper in a church steeple, when suddenly the steeple was hit by a bazooka shell, a tommy gun, and several M1s. The result — no more sniper.

The difference between the "green" man and the veteran in combat is not a matter of fear. The veteran is scared, too. But the difference is that in spite of his fear the veteran will be able to size up the situation and react in the best way possible, while the "greenhorn" is too confused and inexperienced to know how to react. I can tell you this though, the "green man" learns very fast or he becomes very dead. There is a lot of truth in the saying about "the quick and the dead." The man in combat has three things that will help keep him alive: to know his job, to play percentages, and to have a hell of a lot of luck.

When we ran into the Platoon Lieutenant and Sergeant Morris, we stepped into a building in order to get organized to go on the patrol. The Lieutenant asked how I liked combat.

"Not worth a damn, sir."

Just as we were about to depart on the patrol, the Intelligence Officer (another Lieutenant) came stepping down the street with three captured prisoners. He had decided that if he was going to get any prisoners for questioning that he would have to capture them for himself, and he looked real proud that he had been so successful. It was already becoming apparent that this was to be a battle of the "black flag," no quarter asked and no quarter given, "take no prisoners." The S-2 brought his prisoners into the building where we were standing. As they passed through the door, one of the men inside offered to take the "sons-of-bitches" off the Lieutenant's hands. "We'll take them out back and you won't have to worry about them anymore."

All the men in the room, with the exception of Cap and me, began to push and shove to take the captives out and kill them. But the S-2 became very upset and stated that he needed these men for interrogation and meant for them to be left alone. Suddenly the big arrogant German soldier who seemed to be their leader (he was obviously SS) said to Sergeant Morris, "Gimme a cigarette!"

Morris's hand snaked out and snatched a pack of Phillip Morris out of the kraut's shirt pocket, and he said, "I want you to tell me what in the hell is wrong with Phillip Morris!" (He knew that this kraut had looted these American cigarettes off a dead GI.)

The offensive kraut said, "I don't like Phillip Morris, I like Luckies."

That's when all hell broke loose. I don't think that Sergeant Morris really meant to harm the Germans, but the others in the room clearly had that in mind. There was a lot of bitter cussing and carrying on, for these men of the 101st were remembering Malmédy and all the other American GIs who had fallen in this senseless effort that Hitler had launched. I was somewhat shocked by all this determination to shoot prisoners, but I was to learn that combat does bad things to good men. Combat is not fought and won by little boys in knee pants and lace collars. To survive in combat, most men have to get themselves down to the same brute level of the enemy. Anyone who tries to hold on to the highest level of civilized society will either wind up in Section 8 — a physical or mental discharge — or perhaps dead.

In the Battle of Bastogne, for example, a big shell had landed just across the street from the building I was in, and a GI I didn't know came in with a grin on his face, announcing that an officer had been killed. This GI had casually strolled across the street and urinated on the dead man's head saying, "Good for you, you son-of-a-bitch, I'm glad you got yours." I didn't know the officer or the GI who had done this, although many actions committed during combat would be shocking to civilians. I don't believe that most combat men would be particularly shocked. It seems that the men who were under this particular officer hated him, and thus there is a moral here. If you're not a good, tough, square-shooter, don't be a combat officer. And if you are a stinker, and are going to be a combat officer, it would be a damned good idea to get yourself unstunk before you get to combat. Combat men do not waste much sympathy on a rat. Yet, the same GI who had committed this act at any other time might well have risked his life to save this officer, explaining that "somebody had to save the old son-of-a-bitch." Combat is a very peculiar circumstance and likewise does peculiar things to the men so engaged.

After the furor over what to do with the German prisoners had died down, we set out on our patrol. We went to the north end of Noville, turned due left and went across a pasture, down one hill, then up another towards a village about 500 or 600 yards away. A big black enemy tank was off to our right about 150 to 200 yards, engaged in a gun duel with one of our tank destroyers that was sitting at the north end of Noville. No one seemed to be concerned that it was unusual for us to be out crossing the meadow in plain sight and within range of this tank. All the gunner had to do was turn his turret around a little and mow us down like rats.

Sergeant Morris was at the head of the patrol and he was running, and I kept yelling at him to know why in the hell he didn't walk. We had been marching all day with all this equipment on our backs and the bursts of adrenaline and their after-effects had me so weak I could hardly move. I was tired, but he kept us running in spurts and he was right. Sometimes I think a "green" man in his first two days of combat is about 90 percent stupid. As we approached another village, I saw a small group of men go behind a building, and I yelled at Sergeant Morris that he had better slow down because they might be the enemy. But he must have had a clearer vision than I had because he kept running. I hurried to catch up, and we were closely bunched together when we stepped around the corner of the building. I expected us to have a knock-down shoot-out on the spot, but lucky for us it was a Lieutenant and patrol from the company we were going to contact. They stopped for us to catch up with them, and just as we did so an old Belgian man came out of his house with a heart-wrenching look of gratitude on his face. In his hands he held a loaf of bread and a bottle of wine. He offered it to us with deep emotion. A few of the men took a piece of bread and a swig of the wine. As for me, those K-ration eggs and biscuits that I had eaten that morning were still settling in my stomach, and not too well.

We combined our patrols and moved down the road toward the south until we reached the end of the village. We then went back across the field, up the side of a hill, and turned back north so that we could go back to the same route that we had taken out of Noville. As we traveled along the hillside, moving generally toward the black German tank that was still firing toward the town, the Lieutenant was in front and I was in the rear, about 15 yards behind the next soldier. Suddenly, from somewhere in the vicinity of that tank a machine gun cut loose about two or three feet above my head. High-powered bullets make an explosive popping sound as they go by. You can tell their distance by the loudness of the pop, and you can also see tracers as they pass by. As things happen, you don't have time to think, but get flashes that cover the whole situation. I knew if that gunman depressed the barrel of his machine gun just the slightest bit he would cut me to smithereens. I figured that if he lowered his sights a little, he would knock me off and then would sweep the entire patrol. I was the last man, and if I got killed he would eliminate the rest of the patrol before they had any warning. As I tumbled to the ground, I made sure that I landed as flat as possible and yelled at the others. The Lieutenant in front yelled, without even looking back, "Ah, come on, he's not shooting at you." Even though I thought I might be dead in seconds, his remark made me see red. I yelled back, "Hell, no, he's not shooting at you, he's shooting at me." That was my first anger reaction in combat and I found that anger is just about the best friend a soldier ever has. Fear without anger breeds apathy, but anger brings out determination and perseverance.

As I lay there, the gunner depressed the barrel of his machine gun until the bullets were passing over my head from a distance of six to twelve inches. The popping of the bullets was so loud it seemed they would burst my eardrum, and I could see the tracers as they zipped past my head. I thought I was a goner at first, but the stream of bullets seemed to stabilize just above me, and this gave me hope that being on this hillside was fooling the gunner into thinking he was right on target. I thought to myself that if he ever stopped shooting he would probably watch me for a few seconds, and if I didn't move, he would look elsewhere for another target. I'll never know why he shot at only me, unless he thought I might be an officer. But after what seemed like an eternity, the machine gun suddenly stopped. I lay perfectly still for about 15 or 20 seconds, then I sprang to my feet all in one motion and ran for the edge of the woods about 20 or 30 yards away. I jumped over a rusty barbed-wire fence at the edge of the woods and went into the trees. I ran along the inside the woods and caught the patrol as it turned back toward Noville.

When we got back into Noville, all the shooting had stopped except for some sporadic shelling. The Sergeant and Lieutenant began making plans for the night as it was by then very late in the afternoon. Some of us went to a building that was the last one in town facing the enemy. There was a basement in the building and within the basement was a small room that seemed to have been used for storage. The main part of the basement was the same size as the whole building and the back part didn't even have any space upstairs but went all the way to the roof. We piled up in the little storage room for the night, but guards had to be posted. I caught two shifts that night, one real early and one about two o'clock in the morning. Standing my first guard was a frightening situation; although I knew the Germans and the GIs were all over the countryside, there was not a sound of a man anywhere in this foggy blackness. All that I heard was the low-pitched crackles and pops of a building smoldering down the street. The slowing fire actually looked warm and cheerful, and it would have been nice to walk over and warm myself, but I stayed in the doorway shivering, cold, and afraid.

The Germans were somewhere out there in the darkness, and they weren't ready to give up yet. I felt like we were involved in a game of cat and mouse. When I caught my next shift, sometime around 2 a.m., it was a little different. This time there was plenty of sound. Down the road where the krauts were, it sounded like a bunch of drunks on Saturday afternoon. They were yelling and whooping and someone would start up a tank and make it sound like a teenager trying to scratch off at the drive-in. This went on until just before daybreak, and later into the morning. A German prisoner told me that he could really fight if he had about three or four good shots of booze just before a battle. I believed him. Just before daybreak, there was a thick pea soup fog and it was totally unpenetrable. We heard the German tanks start up and begin to move toward us. This was it.

Chapter Four

Armageddon

SO MANY GERMAN TANKS moved toward Noville that the ground actually trembled. And there we were, as far as I knew, with no armored support except two or three tank destroyers. Although our boys were good, it was too much to expect them to take on this whole convoy of enemy tanks bearing down on us.

There was a lot of activity going on in the basement now. Sergeant Morris was trying to get everyone assigned to some place of deployment. At first, he told me to come upstairs with some other guys, then he changed his mind and told me to stay down in the basement with a Sergeant that I barely knew. In this confined room there was a small window that faced the highway, and we were trying to fire the bazooka from this window.

When Sergeant Morris had gotten everyone paired up and in some semblance of organization, they all left and went upstairs. He had split Cap and me and I was left as ammo man for the Sergeant. As they left, the Sergeant said, "Okay, Simms, load me up." Somehow I got a rocket out of my bag, pulled the safety pin, placed it in the bazooka and wired it up without dropping it or collapsing. The tanks were getting closer and it was a terrible and fearsome sound, as the night was so dark and foggy that no one could see anything. Anxiety flooded over me like I have never felt before.

The highway was mined about 30 to 50 yards from our building, and the little basement window would be perfect for clear observation in that direction if it had been lighter and no fog, but we could not see two feet beyond the window. The German planning for the Battle of the Bulge had been based on this kind of weather.

The Sergeant pointed the bazooka out the window, and because the room was so narrow it made rocket firing marginal at best. So I leaned up against the wall next to the window to escape the bounce of the back blast off the other wall. The lead tank came up the highway and drove right into the mined roadway. A mine blew up with a thundering roar. The Sergeant let out an almost maniacal laugh and said, "That will fix them sons-of-bitches!" But it didn't. The tank growled around again and hit another mine and the Sergeant would laugh some more. This went on until the tank had exploded all the mines and it still wasn't knocked out.

By that time, the bazooka rocket looked about as big as a match head. The Sergeant was trying to get a bead on the tank by sound, since we couldn't see anything. Every time he would get the bazooka lined up and ready to fire, the tank would grunt and growl, with the sound coming from a slightly different place. This cat-and-mouse game went on for a few minutes, when suddenly a big shell came in and hit the roof of our building. It seemed as if the structure would have shaken to pieces, but it didn't. At this instant I heard Sergeant Morris let out with an agonized scream, which I soon recognized as peculiar to all men hit by shell fragments. The situation crystalized in my mind immediately, and I knew I could die at any moment.

From that day on, I have known what it feels like to anticipate death. The mechanical part of dying is of no consequence, since it is just a process of losing consciousness. Many people have been unconscious, but yet have recovered. Some people, seemingly not so serious, may drift into a coma and die. Since I have been unconscious a number of times from a variety of reasons, I know what this is like. What it really feels like to die is to know ahead of time that it will happen, and you have to wait, for it to occur.

I was convinced I was going to die because this enemy attack appeared to be a massive frontal assault with unlimited armor and troops. As far as I knew, we had virtually no armor. I fully expected these tanks to pull up close, throw a few high explosive shells through the windows of the house, and move on. If we were not all dead after that, the following wave of infantry with grenades and automatic weapons would finish the butchery.

It is a long story why things didn't happen that way, and somewhat irrelevant. The main point for me at that time was that the way I saw it, death was inevitable. Some men go through combat without going through this experience, because as long as you believe there is a chance, you don't have this feeling. I had many close calls in combat, but this was the only time when I lost all hope. Most combat men are extremely honest in relating these experiences. If they haven't experienced this they will say, "I don't think I ever got to that point." But, a combat veteran who has experienced this condition will recognize it, and virtually all with whom I have discussed this will tell the same story.

Once it became apparent that we might be killed right then and there, I was seized by a terrible sinking feeling that almost knocked me out. I felt physically sick and was terrified that I would lose control of myself and be reduced to a blubbering coward. Thankfully, the reserve strength comes to the rescue at times like this, and even though a man faces death, he has a desire to die with dignity. In desperation, I asked the Sergeant if he had ever been sick in combat, and he said, "Hell, yes, nearly every new man that goes into combat is sick sooner or later; it will go away in a little while."

Surprisingly enough it did, and I got myself under control. This in no way relieves the dread and fear of dying, but it helps a little to know you can stand there and accept it like a man. That old saying that a man's life flashes before him at the moment of imminent death is a lot of hogwash. My life, good or bad, had no influence on my feelings. It simply did not enter my mind. The main feeling I had was a numb overwhelming dread of oblivion. The fear or hope of the hereafter seemed to be very remote and unconcerned with the present. I thought briefly of home and the good life that might have lay ahead for me. I had the feeling that the solar system and the universe would keep spinning on forever, but I would not get to see any of it. I knew that everyone has to die, but that when a person lives out a normal life span, nature somehow conditions him to accept it. When a healthy young person is suddenly put in this position, he is not ready to accept his death as a normal process.

My only alternatives to this fate — for all soldiers in combat have to think of alternatives — were to make the best judgment, to select the best position possible, and to do everything that will give the best chance to execute my job and still stay alive. The alternative was that in all the darkness, noise, and confusion I could easily slip out the door of this little room, hurry up the stairs, out the back door, and down a back alley to the other end of town, and then I could pretend to be lost in all the confusion. Inasmuch as everyone in that building would surely be killed, there would be no witnesses. But there was only one hitch to this, as I knew. Just the thought of committing such an act filled me with revulsion. I believe the guilt of "running away" would be something like committing psychological suicide. I used to look down on people who had "Better Death than Dishonor" tattooed on an arm, but I can't any more. Maybe some who wear that emblem are childish and "corny," but I found out the hard way that the phrase's meaning is deeper in most of us than we think.

Because I was in no way tempted to run away, I found myself in the unhappy position of literally choosing to die. If you don't think that is earthshaking, try it sometime. I can promise you that you'll never be the same again.

All these thoughts took only a few seconds, and in the meantime the Sergeant was still trying to get a bead on one of those tanks, but because of the fog and darkness it was like a blind man trying to find a needle in a haystack.

Another group came down into the basement, and they had a medic with them. They were carrying Sergeant Morris and helping another wounded boy. It was getting light enough to see a little, although the fog still reduced visibility almost to zero. The medic dressed Sergeant Morris's wound and gave him a shot of morphine. A large piece of shell fragment had gone into his back, almost passing completely through him, but was visibly pouched up under the skin of his abdomen. It looked to be roughly an inch to an inch and a half square and it had gone through flat-sided. I figured he was a goner, and soon was unconscious and became as pale and waxy-looking as a corpse. The other boy who was wounded had his eyeball knocked out; it was hanging down on his cheek in a bloody mess. Terrible eye injuries do not always respond to morphine as well as the majority of other wounds, and this boy was having a very rough time, but he was trying hard to be as brave.

After they brought the wounded into the small room, it was impossible to fire the bazooka there since the back blast would endanger their welfare. While we were in the process of taking care of them, a tank had pulled up in front of the building and was sending machine-gun fire in a deadly hail down the street. Another had pulled out in the back of the building and was spraying lead all over the place. When they got the wounded settled, the Sergeant said, "Okay, Simms, we will have to go upstairs and get 'em now."

Well, I knew to do that we would be committing suicide because of the arrangement of the building. In order to get a shot at either tank we would have to step right out in front of them in the line of fire of their machine guns. I never expected us to even get off one rocket. I had already chosen to die once that morning and with only briefest reprieve, I was now expected to deliberately commit suicide. But then I had already had that battle with myself, so I picked up my ammo bag and without a word I followed the Sergeant across the big room.

As we gradually started inching up the stairs, he suddenly paused. "Wait just a minute, I'm going back in there and see if I can get a grenade or two off some of those wounded guys." I waited for about a minute, but didn't feel comfortable where I was, so I moved over against the front wall of the basement. I stood very still for two or three minutes, wondering why the Sergeant had not come back, then decided to go back to the little room and see what was holding him up. Taking a long stealthy step down the stairs, a burst of machine gun fire hit the wall exactly where I had been standing. I looked back and the wall looked as if you had sprinkled it with pepper. This taught me a very valuable lesson; just because the enemy can't see you doesn't mean he can't hit you. I continued back down to the small room and when I entered, the Sergeant made no mention of going back up. I noticed a Lieutenant was among the group in the room, and I suppose that the Sergeant had conferred with the officer on the matter and they considered it useless for the time being.

I sat down against the wall and tried to figure out how civilized people could ever get themselves into such a mess, and began to realize that I was cold. My clothes were still damp from falling in a little stream the day before. The body goes through a tremendous strain in adjusting to combat and sheer terror had made me unaware of any discomfort.

About this time, one of the men suggested we might as well eat as it might be the last chance we would get. I didn't know whether he meant that day or forever, and I didn't ask! Food was the farthest thing from my mind; to hell with the last meal. But I felt that I had to be as game as the rest, so I broke open my K-ration and when I opened the can it contained cold greasy potted meat. I listened to those tanks firing out there. I looked at that bloody eyeball hanging on that boy's cheek. I looked at that greasy mess in that can, and all I could do was back my ears and dig in. In a desperate attempt to get the K-ration down and appear as casual as possible, I would find myself silently saying, "Stay down, you greasy son-of-a-bitch!" even though my "gozzle" was jumping up and down like a yo-yo.

After I ate, for the lack of something to do I eased out into the big room. I thought that if there was a table or some kind of equipment we could move near the window at the back, we might possibly be able to get the bazooka high enough to get a shot at the tank. The bottom of the windows were about eight feet from the floor and it would require something high and steady enough in order to get a good shot. To shoot haphazardly would do more harm than good, and might even hit some of our men out there somewhere. To fire from the floor level we would have to fire from the farthest side of the big room where we could just barely see his turret. To secure a hit the bazooka shell would have to clear the bottom of the window, by about an inch, go through the broken pane of the window; if it was aimed too high, it would miss the tank altogether. But if it didn't thread that "keyhole," it would explode in the room — and no one likes for one of those things to go bang in the same room with him!

However, the room had absolutely nothing we could use to stand on, so I gave up on that. Had I found something, I would have told the Sergeant and let him use his own judgment. I went back in the little room to sweat it out and wait for what I now hoped would be some kind of a break. The Lieutenant called periodically on his radio to ask what the current condition was, and the answer was always the same: "Hold your position until further orders." In between these calls the Lieutenant would sit expressionless, and I would wonder if he was scared to death; but then he would again call on the radio, and I could tell that he was merely practicing what I was to learn later — the maddening patience that combat men have to develop.

Soon after I went back into the room, he called for some artillery to try to get in on those tanks. He told them our position and said, "Overshoot a little and I'll walk you back." In seconds, a shell screamed over and landed about 100 yards down the highway. The Lieutenant said, "Back it up about 50 yards," and in a few seconds another shell screamed overhead and landed about halfway between us and the first hit. The Lieutenant said, "Back up another 50 yards," and almost immediately a shell screamed in that sounded as if it would surely hit the building. It barely cleared the roof and hit just outside the wall. The building shifted up and down and the Lieutenant said, "Whew, that was a little too damned close." He told them to raise it a few yards and throw in a few, but it was useless because the tanks were too close to us.

In a little while a machine gun opened up in the street in front of the building. Since we had not heard another tank drive up, this meant only one thing — infantry. The Lieutenant told us almost immediately to get that guy. We all fanned out into the big room and scattered around covering each other and trying to make sure that no German infantry caught us off guard. Some of the more experienced men were trying to locate a line of vision so that they could pick off the machine gunner. As we were silently watching and looking, I suddenly heard something that caused me to cock my head and look around. Every man in the room had his head turned to one side, listening intently, some with faint smiles on their faces. There was no infantry machine gun out there. The gun was a quarter of a mile down the road. As the bullets came down the street breaking the sound barrier, the echo from the arrangement of the buildings had fooled us all, including the Lieutenant.

Finally the Lieutenant told a soldier to get a line on the tank out front. We already had investigated this for firing the bazooka, and the place from which you could get a narrow view of the tank was pretty marginal. The main prohibiting factor was a wall extension sticking out into the room at the bottom of the stairs. When you were in a position to see a small part of the tank, the back end of the bazooka was almost against this extended wall. This would cause the man firing a bazooka to be cooked to a crisp!

The soldier designated by the Lieutenant went out into the big room, crouched down, and darted across to the stairs. Because I had already familiarized myself with the situation out in the larger room, I went with him to cover him from behind. When we got to the stairs I told him that the tank out back had almost gotten me, and if I saw its turret move I would knock him over behind this abutment.

I dared not even watch as he prepared to fire, because if the enemy soldier slipped up to the back window I had to be ready, and if the tank tur-ret moved I had to get us under cover. With me watching from behind, he could concentrate on trying to shoot. He went up to the third step, then leaned from side to side, shifting his feet a bit until he was satisfied with his position. Suddenly he raised his rifle, steadied, and fired. He slowly lowered his rifle, gave a disgusted chuckle. "Missed the son-of-a-bitch."

He swayed back and forth again lining himself up with the openings. He quickly raised his rifle again, fired, and lowering his rifle said, "Got him." By then the tank had stopped firing and within ten seconds the motor started, and the tank turned and left; as it did, the one behind the house started up and also left. As far as I could tell there were about two other tanks nearby, and they rumbled away as well.

"For the lack of a nail the shoe was lost." There we were pinned down virtually helpless. There had been no way to fight back, to get at the tanks with the bazooka, and then the Lieutenant's idea and one bullet sent them packing. We were elated at this state of events because now deployment into a different position would give us a chance to be more effective. The orders over the radio still told us to hold our positions until further orders.

When the tanks were gone, the medics took the boy whose eye had been knocked out and left the building on the run. There was no way that he could take Sergeant Morris with him, so now the sole responsibility for Morris having a remote chance at life rested squarely on the rest of us. The responsibility for a wounded and helpless comrade certainly has an effect on the combat man's mobility and also on his conscience.

The German tanks had only been gone a few minutes when we heard American tanks coming from the same direction. We thought that this was the real reason the German tanks withdrew.

"Listen to those damned fifties talking." We were overjoyed because we thought that somehow we had gotten a big tank reinforcement.

The American tanks came up to our building, took the identical posi-tions that had been occupied by the German tanks, and began to pour on the lead in the same manner. "Hell, there's something wrong here," some-one shouted. The Lieutenant got on the radio and told his superiors, "There are some Sherman tanks out here and they're acting mighty pecu-liar." The word came back, "Those are captured American tanks. Shoot the hell out of them if you can."

The American kraut-driven tanks stayed only a short while, then pulled out and left. Finally, orders came for us to pull back to the other end of town. This was an enormous relief for me, because anything would beat being penned up in a building from which it was impossible to fight back.

The first order of business was to carry Sergeant Morris with us. We had four men on the stretcher, and we helped carry each other's equipment so that the men carrying the stretcher would have a lighter load. We went up the stairs and out the back door in a frantic run. I expected to see dead cows everywhere because during all the shooting Holsteins were wandering around out there bawling and bellowing. I saw no cows, but there was a dead white hog lying there.

When we took the back-alley route to go to the other end of town, we found that we were blocked by a seven-foot smooth plank wall. Getting Sergeant Morris over this presented a problem. We raised the front handles of the stretcher until they rested on the wall. At the same time, some of the men held the rear handles as high as they could. Amongst all this frantic confusion, Sergeant Morris was startled and opened his eyes and looked straight at me; then he slipped back into unconsciousness. When the front handles were placed on top of the wall, some of us began to scramble over. With all the equipment I was carrying it was like trying to swim with lead weights. As a few of us climbed over, we slipped the stretcher forward until the back handles rested on the wall, then the others scrambled over and we set off for the opposite end of town at a dead run.

When we got near our destination we ran into quite a few American tanks, and I wondered why they hadn't moved out and taken on the kraut tanks. It was only later that I realized that what little armor we had needed to be hoarded carefully until that time when there was no alternative. If our tanks had been recklessly committed and lost, we all would have been dead ducks.

The Battle of Bastogne was won partly on generalship. Instead of taking a defensive position, we went on the attack so aggressively that the Germans began to probe for weak places, and that was their fatal mistake. If the enemy had concentrated all of its resources into a massive frontal assault, the final result would have been different; but the aggressive attack we had made at the outset caused him to hesitate, and "he who hesitates is lost."

When we reached the edge of town, we found out the Germans had tried to out-flank and encircle our battalion, and that was the reason why the tanks that had pinned us down had not tried to advance. The tanks were merely diversionary, and the reason they did not put high-explosive shells into our building began to make sense. The krauts did not want us dead, they just wanted us hemmed in. If they had sent shells into the building it would have been observed, and if our side had seen that we were all being killed, then the artillery would have moved right on top of the kraut tanks. Because their primary mission was to keep us pinned down while their encirclement attempt was being made, they did not want to kill us just yet. If the encirclement of the battalion had succeeded, then it would have been a very different story.

When we reached the south end of town, we ran up to a tank that was parked in the middle of the road. We asked the tank commander if this tank was going to the rear that night. He said it would, so we asked permission to lash Sergeant Morris's stretcher to the tank so that he could be taken rearward. We placed the stretcher crosswise on the back of the tank and secured it so that Sergeant Morris would not fall off.

About the time we arrived at that side of town, Cappaletti came running up and we were reunited. It seems as if he had already been sent out of the building before Sergeant Morris got hit, and he had been in another part of the town, unaware of what had taken place in our position. An officer filled us in on the overall situation and told us that an area was being cleared to the rear so that we could withdraw through the lines of one of our other battalions. He told us it was our duty to fight a rear-guard action if the Germans tried to come in before we could withdraw.

Cap and I took turns digging and tried to keep on top of the situation. Every few minutes the tank on which Sergeant Morris was tied would send a burst of .50-caliber machine-gun fire right down main street and on out toward the krauts. Those deafening bullets would go right over Sergeant Morris's body, but he slept peacefully through it all. We had about 300 to 400 dead and wounded, and some of the wounded had no one left to carry them out, so the Germans butchered them on the spot.

Finally, someone gave the word that we were to move out and told us to get into a half-track. We loaded up and moved toward the rear. One of the armored infantry boys said to me, "Man, you all have some good officers." I asked what he meant and he told me that the Lieutenant had scraped together a little rag-tag bunch of men that included both paratrooper and armored infantry. They were stealthily moving along when

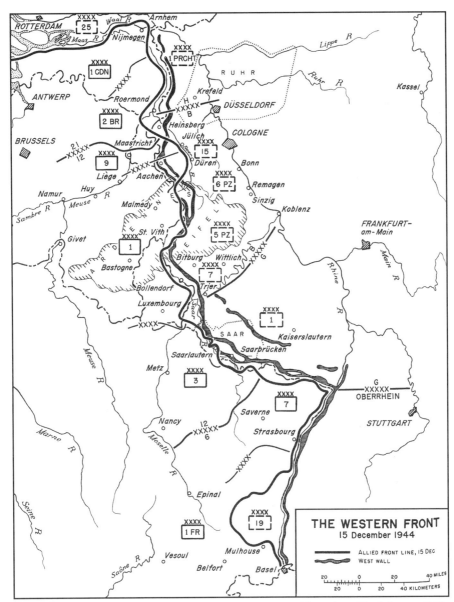

From **United States Army in World War II, The European Theater of Operations. The Ardennes: Battle of the Bulge**, by Hugh M. Cole (Washington, D.C.: Office of the Chief of Military History, U.S. Army, 1965), 52

From *United States Army in World War II, The European Theater of Operations. The Ardennes: Battle of the Bulge,* by Hugh M. Cole (Washington, D.C.: Office of the Chief of Military History, U.S. Army, 1965), 473

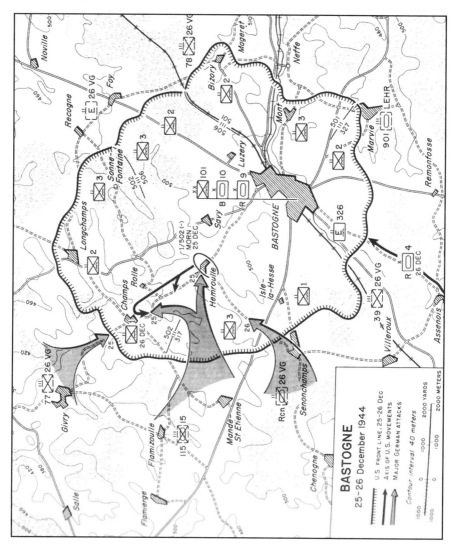

BASTOGNE
25–26 December 1944

U.S. FRONT LINE, 25-26 DEC
AXIS OF U.S. MOVEMENTS
MAJOR GERMAN ATTACKS

Contour interval 40 meters

0   1000   2000 YARDS
0   1000   2000 METERS

Bastogne, a quiet village in the Belgian Ardennes, in December 1944. The success of the German attack depended largely on its capture, but it ultimately failed due to American "sheer guts" and combat intelligence.
From The Epic of the 101st Airborne: A Pictorial Record of a Great Fighting Team (101st Airborne Division, 1945)

German prisoners of war being marched to the rear by an American infantryman, December 1944.
U.S. Army photo courtesy Dwight D. Eisenhower Library, Abilene, KS

An American Sherman tank passing an incapacitated German Panzer tank during the Battle of the Bulge.
U.S. Army photo courtesy Dwight D. Eisenhower Library, Abilene, KS

A destroyed German tank hit hard enough that the turret blew off and is upside down in the snow, December 1944. *U.S. Army photo courtesy Dwight D. Eisenhower Library, Abilene, KS*

An American soldier reloading his rifle in front of dead German soldiers at the Battle of the Bulge. *U.S. Army photo courtesy Dwight D. Eisenhower Library, Abilene, KS*

American medics helping wounded Belgian children, December 1944. *U.S. Army photo courtesy Dwight D. Eisenhower Library, Abilene, KS*

A dead German soldier at the Battle of the Bulge. *U.S. Army photo courtesy Dwight D. Eisenhower Library, Abilene, KS*

they spotted a squad of German infantry. The Lieutenant whispered to them to count off from each end so that no shots would be unaccounted for. When everyone was ready, the Lieutenant told them to get down on one knee so as to have steady aim. When everyone was in place, the Lieutenant gave the order to fire and the German squad was instantly wiped out. The infantryman said the Lieutenant made it look so easy it was like shooting fish in a barrel.

We had a German prisoner in the half-track with us. He had been shot through the calf of his leg, but was not complaining. In fact, I believe he was relieved to be captured. He couldn't speak English, and I couldn't speak German, but he somehow communicated his age to be 17 years old, and that he had been in the service since September.

Suddenly, another soldier seized the German kid by the arm and started to relieve him of his wrist watch. I was surprised to find myself saying, "Leave the damn boy alone." I was even more surprised when three or four more men in the half-track echoed my words and told this guy, "Let him keep the damned watch." The soldier backed off without protest. I knew that just as quick as the prisoner got to a rear area some guard would lift his watch, but in my first 24 hours of combat I had seen so much death, blood, and fear that it only seemed fair to show a little compassion.

Two Sherman tanks on the main highway had been knocked out and were still smoldering. In the late afternoon haziness, they cast an eerie glow as they burned silently. We were traveling parallel to the highway because tanks were blocking the road. Presently we came upon a jeep driven by a medical Captain. On this jeep were two litter cases, one lashed across the hood and the other across the back seat. The man on the back litter was receiving plasma from a bottle secured to an upright stand. The jeep was hopelessly stuck in the mud with one side buried up to the axle. As we drove up, the half-track driver stopped so that we could push the jeep out of the mud.

As we neared this situation, our eyes caught sight of a young paratrooper lying face down on the ground, stone-dead. He looked for all the world just like someone who had had a big Sunday dinner and was sprawled crosswise on a bed taking a nap. We piled out of the half-track and proceeded to push the jeep out of the mud. The two wounded boys were jostled about somewhat, but they never uttered a word of pain or protest. We soon had the jeep out, and the medical Captain roared away with his responsibilities.

Shells were screaming overhead in every direction, and it was a grim and fearsome time. As we got back into the half-track my eyes were drawn again to the dead paratrooper. I imagined that his family would be discussing the last letter they had received from him, without realizing that he was already dead. I am sure this happened often as the chaos of battle caused many delays in communications. In a few days they would receive a telegram that would bear the most bitter news that parents ever have to know: "The War Department regrets to inform you . . . ."

As we pulled away, the fog was settling in and it was almost dark, but I kept looking back at the dead kid. He looked so relaxed, so cold, so young, so alone, and so *finally* dead. As long as a soldier has a wounded comrade in his keep, he will jeopardize his chances to fight, but when the welfare of the group is at stake, in "No Man's Land," the dead have to take their own chances.

Chapter Five

The Bait

WE RODE ON FOR SOME distance in the half-track, and I was not even aware of passing through the line that had been set up by one of our other battalions. Finally, we came out on the highway abreast of a small group of houses. The half-track stopped and someone said, "Everybody off, this is as far as we go!" Night was falling, and there was a furious firefight going on over to the northeast. Artillery shells were screaming overhead from every direction, and I was so disoriented that I could hardly identify where they were coming from. We had arrived at night and hadn't seen the sun in days; therefore, direction meant nothing. Even if I had had access to a map, it wouldn't have cleared up a lot of the confusion.

We unloaded and no time was wasted in assigning guard and sentry duty. Guards were sent out in every direction and each man soon knew his post and time. A casual conversation developed between another soldier and myself. I was aware he had been in combat before and he knew that I was a "green soldier." He figured that all "green" men in rough combat are a bit shook up the first few days, and said to me, "How would you like to get out of here?"

"What man in his right mind wouldn't like to get out of here?" I answered.

"Well, we can get out," he told me.

I knew there had to be a catch, but out of curiosity I asked, "How?"

"All we have to do in the morning is approach a medic and pretend to be sick at the stomach, spit up a little — you can spit up, can't you?" I told him I didn't think so. But he kept explaining his scheme, then asked, "What do you think about it?"

I was really surprised not only at my answer but at how quick I gave it. "If I had a million dollars, and if I thought it would stop this mess, I would give the money over in a minute and never look back; but I just can't go that route."

"Well, you think about it tonight," he said, "and let me know in the morning if you've changed your mind, because whether you go with me or not, I'm getting out of here."

Well, that night I thought about it, as I stood my hitch on sentry and later lying in a barn trying to get sleep that wouldn't come. I was never in doubt about whether or not I would try the scheme, but what bothered me was that the decisions concerning life or death seemed to keep coming without end. A man is constantly in a struggle for his honor and self-respect, which are a result of his actions. This is not just my dilemma, but applies to all men in combat. And when a man faces up to these questions with regard to his behavior during combat, the decisions that come about later in civilian life seem trivial in comparison.

The next morning we were called out. Our battalion had been shot to hell, and we were organized into new groups. The soldier who had talked to me earlier happened to be put in my group. We were supposed to be going somewhere, but I didn't have the slightest idea where. We were told that my group was to go ahead and the other group was to stay and guard headquarters. About the time this got straightened out, I saw a medic walk up. The soldier that had approached me the night before caught my eye and raised his eyebrows. I slightly shook my head "No," and he shrugged his shoulders and walked over to the medic. I watched him go into his act.

He talked in earnest for a little bit, while the medic listened intently. In a little while they both turned and walked to the rear.

We were ready to move out when one of the noncoms told another noncom that the "sick man" had gone. This made my group one man short, so the men who had originally been assigned to guard headquarters were substituted for my group and we were left behind to guard.

The battalion — what was left of it — moved out. A group of about seven or eight of us were left to see that no German task force would breach the lines and take our headquarters. We weren't assigned a formal place of post, instead we just roamed about, keeping our eyes peeled for anything that might occur.

As some of us were standing in the street, a noncom came out of a building and said, "Hey, do any of you know a GI named Rodriguez?" I said, "Yes, I know someone by that name." I didn't know at that time that almost every other Mexican-American person was named Rodriguez.

The noncom said, "What about coming around back of the building and identifying a body?" I went around back and there lay a boy with about a quarter of the left front part of his head blown away. The body looked a great deal like the Rodriguez I knew, but I told the noncom that I couldn't be 100 percent sure. The Rodriguez I knew was a short and funny guy who was nearly always smiling or laughing. He had a typical Mexican accent and was very easy to get along with. I had asked him one time how the hell Mexicans could stand all that hot food. He replied, "It is good for the stomock." I said, "Hell, it will burn your stomach up." He answered, "You never heard of a Mexican with stomock trobble, have you?"

I returned to the others in the street, and the first man I met was Rodriguez, bouncing along, grinning for all the world like he was going down Main Street, USA. I told him, "Get the hell behind that building and lie down; you're dead. I just identified your body!"

Rodriguez laughed and replied, "I can ashoor you that I am not dead. I was caught behind the German lines yesterday and when I was trying to make my way back it got dark and I came to a barn, so I just went up in the hay and slept. When morning came I got up and came on back."

"Well, how'd you get through the kraut lines?" I asked.

He replied, "I did not see any Germans."

As we patrolled the area keeping a lookout for any trouble, I heard the name "Lieutenant Sims" addressed to a small quick-moving Lieutenant. I had heard stories about this Lieutenant. Agy told me that when they were in Holland, battling alongside the British, the boys in the 506th suddenly found themselves about half a mile ahead of them. The Germans aren't stupid and they noticed this as well, so they immediately tried to out-flank the 506th boys and wedge in-between the Americans and the British. When the Americans saw what was going on, they gave the order to withdraw to a point even with the British. When the order was given, everyone took off to the rear since this is the quickest way that a gap can best be closed. Lieutenant Sims didn't have any weight to carry except a carbine and a light pack and he said he was running as he had never run before. About this time, a big raw hillbilly carrying a completely assembled machine gun on his shoulder passed Lieutenant Sims like he was standing still. As he went by, he said, "Gawd damn, Lieutenant, you better run. They a'comin'."

As we waited around that morning, word was passed that Sergeant Morris had died, and I wondered whether all the concern and effort the day before had been worth it. I wondered if anything was worth it. At least, though, his body was back where it could be taken care of. A long time after that, one of the men in the company received a letter from Sergeant Morris! It seems as if the records got fouled up in all the wartime confusion, and a week after his family had a memorial service for him, he walked up to his home in the States and knocked on the door! If I remember correctly, the doctors had to remove 25 inches of his intestines, and he still lived. He didn't know that he had been lashed onto that tank with a .50-caliber machine gun talking right over his body.

While we stood in the street a German automatic weapon suddenly cut loose just over the hill toward the north. This had a sinister meaning. If the Germans were this far back, it probably meant they had breached the lines and were pouring through like water. Without orders from anyone, we began running toward the sound of the firing. We fell into a skirmish line and waited. Weren't we the big brave American soldiers? If the Germans had indeed breached the lines, then only seven or eight of us were the only ones to take on the whole damned German army.

For a few moments, nothing happened, then a bellowing began that sounded like a big bull in the springtime. The only difference was that this bellowing was coming out "*Kamerad*!" Just then a big curly-headed German topped the hill. He had thrown away his helmet and his gun, and he had his hands on top of his head and was yelling, "*Kamerad! Kamerad!*" He came on down and we took him prisoner.

At that point, we saw the battalion off in the distance. When they got closer, we saw that they had a whole contingent of German prisoners. The night before, a large number of Germans had breached our lines and had dug in behind us. That is where our battalion had gone. Some of the men told me that the Germans were so stubborn that our GIs had to literally overrun them and shoot them pointblank in their holes.

Later, I saw Agy talking to one of the new "green" kids and he was so angry he was shaking. It seems as if this kid who was bazooka ammo man for Agy either had bugged out or had failed to advance with Agy. Agy had looked around for another rocket and he had no ammo man to back him up. I heard Agy say, "Damn your soul, don't you ever do that to me again!" I felt sorry for the kid; he was so scared he was white. But I knew Agy was letting him off pretty easy.

The men disciplined their own in different ways. One guy in our outfit had a reputation for looting, and we had heard that he could shoot a German and loot him before he hit the ground. This guy was in the process of lifting a watch in the midst of battle when he got shot in the leg. Some of the boys said, "We told you you were going to get killed if you didn't cut out that looting!"

When we had been brought up to date on what had happened with our battalion that morning, it suddenly hit me like a ton of bricks. If that guy who turned in sick hadn't gone back, then I would have been in this vicious attack and a bullet with my name on it might have found its home. Because I didn't have to make that attack might very well be the reason I'm living today.

There is nothing unusual about having your life saved by a hero, but to be alive because someone faked being sick is a little out of the ordinary. I have thought much about this since that day. I can't feel too angry at the man. He may have inadvertently saved my life.

Anyway you take it, though, combat does funny things to men, and I guess I realize this more all the time.

Chapter Six

Combat Fatigue

J HAD HEARD OF COMBAT FATIGUE. I didn't really know what caused it, but I was beginning to get an idea. Its final result may be psychological, though the thing that sets up a man for it is physical. In rough combat, a man's adrenal glands start hitting him like a load of bricks. Now to say adrenal is an over-simplification because there are a lot of other factors involved. But when this adrenaline starts pumping, you get kicked up into a high metabolic rate. It would be very simple to say, "So what, control yourself," but the truth is you just can't. The adrenals are not going to pay a damned bit of attention to you; they're going to hit just as hard as the situation demands.

Man or beast is built by nature to either run or fight; but in war man can only fight, and consequently, he may go for days, weeks, or months with his system kicked up to an unnaturally high level.

When the body is stimulated in such a way, sleep doesn't come easily. Some psychoanalyst said that the reason combat men were sleepy was because they were in an impossible situation and they slept to escape. When I read that I laughed. The reason a combat man sleeps is because he is exhausted! A man starts losing sleep anywhere from one to five days after he joins combat. Therefore, he has a big sleep deficit built up at the outset. When he does sleep, its not the deep refreshing slumber of civilian tiredness, but a light rest, without dreams. When your partner taps you on the foot, you immediately know what the situation is and whether he is calling you too soon.

This physiological stress has a tendency to wear the body to a frazzle. Sometimes a man may crouch in a cold, muddy hole for days, with the adrenaline popping in every few minutes; then again, he may be called upon to exert himself physically beyond any believable capacity. At any rate, he is under stress at all times, never gets enough sleep, and therefore he becomes vulnerable to psychological stress.

An over-simplification of how the run-or-fight syndrome sets you up for combat fatigue might be explained like this. If a healthy man walks across a room and painfully hits his shin bone on a chair, he is likely to cuss and holler and generally pitch a fit. If the same man, though, is weak and sick and overcome by nausea and he hits his shin, he is likely to lay down and cry.

On one of these nights, a small group of us was sent out into a pasture, about one-half mile from the Command Post. We set up by a haystack. A very fine mist was falling, the ground was sloppy, and it was cold and miserable. I caught an early shift, and as I stood peering into the dark mist, shells were passing overhead. I think this was the first time I had heard our really "big" stuff. The projectiles came slowly overhead with a whoosh, sounding as if they would fall right on top of me — but they kept plugging along to give some scared German soldier the business.

When I came off my shift, I found out that the World War II sleeping bags were *not* designed for combat men. They zipped down only so far, and when you tried to cram your muddy boots through the opening, the mud would keep them from sliding in easily. After a big struggle, when you finally got in, mud was all over the opening and you were constantly getting the damned stuff in your face. The next day I discarded the sleeping bag and used my blanket and shelter half; together they were better.

But on that particular day, I caught another shift about one o'clock in the morning, and it was cold, wet, and miserable. My feet had not been dry since we had reached Bastogne, and standing in the wet, sloppy mud wasn't helping any. I finally was relieved about 3 a.m. and proceeded to try to struggle back in that damned straight jacket sleeping bag and get some sleep.

When I awoke later, my feet were so cold, they were killing me. I couldn't understand why they felt so numb and detached. I lay there trying to work my toes and get accustomed to the pain. Finally, I stuck my head out of the sleeping bag to discover it was nearly dawn and I was covered with snow.

The day before had been my birthday. Sometime later I received a letter from one of my sisters. She had started the letter by saying, "Well, tonight is your birthday. I hope you have a nice warm place to sleep." The irony of this statement appealed to my "funny bone" and I couldn't help laughing aloud.

As we gathered up our gear and headed across the pasture toward the Command Post, my feet felt as though they were disconnected from my ankles. I wobbled and slipped and stumbled along for about a half mile before feeling began to come back to my feet.

When we got back to headquarters, I overheard one soldier say to another that the Germans had us surrounded and "sealed tight." Another responded, "Who gives a damn. I've never been in combat when I wasn't surrounded."

That afternoon, a small group of us was sent over to a railroad track. Someone had been there before because there were several fox holes already dug. I was assigned to one so small that there was only enough room to squat. I tried to enlarge it, but the roadbed was so full of chunk rock that my entrenching shovel was useless. It was getting colder and the ground around the hole was frozen rock hard. In the bottom of the hole the water and mud was ankle deep. What a hell of a place to sleep that night!

In the afternoon, someone gave the instructions for us not to take off our boots, to dig our holes a little deeper, and to prepare for the worst. The Germans had given the ultimatum for us to surrender or face "annihilation," and General Anthony C. McAuliffe's well-known reply —"Nuts" — was delivered. This was our first introduction to the ongoing drama of war.

Late that afternoon, a Lieutenant in a jeep came out to us with some dry socks. We weren't supposed to take our boots off, but he said he knew that our feet must be getting in a "hell of a shape." "Let one man change at a time, and get your boots off and back on in a hurry."

We did this, but squatting in that mud and water wasn't easy and since our boots were already soaked through, changing socks really didn't do too much good.

I caught an early watch after this and noticed after nightfall that

Brigadier General Anthony C. McAuliffe, Division Artillery Commander, Deputy Division Commander.
*From **The Epic of the 101st Airborne: A Pictorial Record of a Great Fighting Team** (101st Airborne Division, 1945)*

the sky was clearing and the temperature was falling. But I was still too green to catch the significance. All I knew was that I was freezing and that my feet were slowly losing all feeling. It was torture because time seemed to be standing still.

When I finally came off that watch I went to my hole and dug into the mud and water. I pulled my shelter-half over the top of the hole to try to keep out the cold. As I squatted there, with nothing but hours of the same ahead of me, I wondered how I was going to stand it. As miserable as the 33°cold was in that hole, water and mud is warmer than 0° snow!

Eventually, I found myself thinking about my Ml rifle. A click of the safety and a tug of the trigger and my suffering could be over. This option crossed my mind several times while miserably waiting to go on my second watch. Finally, about one o'clock, I caught my second shift, and standing in the snow, the cold seemed to be more than I could bear. When I went back to my hole at about three o'clock and again squatted down in the mud, I realized that I had about four more hours of this torture ahead

*From **The Epic of the 101st Airborne: A Pictorial Record of a Great Fighting Team** (101st Airborne Division, 1945)*

General Anthony C. McAuliffe's response to the German ultimatum that his garrison surrender!
*From **The Epic of the 101st Airborne: A Pictorial Record
of a Great Fighting Team** (101st Airborne Division, 1945)*

of me. My rifle began to be the thing uppermost in my mind, and I found myself caressing the hand guard and thinking about the safety. I didn't want to kill myself, but I was afraid that I was going to do it on impulse.

Suffering does strange things to you. A few days before, I had really wanted to live; but now it seemed that death would be a welcome friend.

About the time this was really getting to me, a young soldier walked by my hole and went over to one occupied by a noncom. This kid didn't look like he could weigh over 110 pounds soaking wet, and he began talking to the Sergeant in a casual manner, as if all of this business wasn't bothering him a bit. All at once I was enraged with myself. "If that little dried up runt can take it, so can I!"

I never thought of taking the easy way out again. A soldier never knows what little incident will help him find his strength.

Somehow, I made it till daylight. Just as the sun was about to come up, I raised up out of my hole and looked back toward Bastogne. Three C-47 Skytrain "Gooney Bird" transports were banking gracefully away and there were several paratroopers in the air. One of the experienced men

James Simms walked through these woods in December 1944. That bitter winter, trench foot and frozen limbs matched casualties from artillery and small arms. Men made crude jackets from blankets and tarpaulins and scarves from the supply chutes.
From The Epic of the 101st Airborne: A Pictorial Record of a Great Fighting Team (101st Airborne Division, 1945)

The men with shovels are preparing for a horrible night. The parents of the man in the foreground could never prepare for the telegram they would receive.   *U.S. Army photo*

said, "They're probably our pathfinders; they'll direct in the planes for air supply."

It was late December of 1944. The clearing sky during the night began to mean something to me now. We gathered up our gear and headed back to the Command Post. By the time we got there, a huge wave of C-47s came roaring in and filled the skies with reinforcements of supplies — ammunition and food to help us hold out a bit longer. The aircraft came over so low that the crew members standing in the door of the planes could easily be seen waving, and we waved back, because this cargo could be life or death for us. I wondered if some of these Army Air Forces guys were ones who had taken their training at Fort Benning when I had been there.

Following the C-47s, the heavy bombers on their way to Germany began coming over, and soon the P-47 Thunderbolt fighter aircraft began working over the Germans and around our perimeter. The heavy bombers were not out of sight of each other from 9 a.m. until about 3 o'clock in the afternoon. Their vapor trails actually put a cloud skim in the sky. The fighter planes were swooping and diving, and the medium bombers were vectoring in on Bastogne from different directions. I told another soldier, "They've routed the whole damn U.S. Army Air Forces over us today!"

This meant something very special. We had been handed a very tough nut to crack, and if we pulled it off many more lives would be saved. And now the people who had called on us to serve were showing us that in no sense had we been forgotten. It made us proud to know that our government and the high command were backing us to the hilt.

Late that afternoon, a terrific fire fight broke out in one sector of the perimeter, and when night fell it was raging furiously. Our battalion had been badly shot up, so we were made "division reserve," meaning that we would be sent to any section that needed beefing up. They assembled us in a building and had us on a 30-minute alert. We had our gear all ready and were staying in a room with a telephone for communication. One of the things that combat men do not like to do is to walk up behind someone else's fire fight at night. You don't know the position of friend or foe, you have no foxhole, and you are not oriented to the terrain — a frightening and sinister situation, and no one in his right mind likes it.

Our field telephone rang and the Lieutenant said, "OK, we're on a fifteen-minute alert." In a few minutes it rang again, and he said,"We're on a five-minute alert." Then he changed back to a 30-minute alert. Over a two-hour period, the tension built higher and higher. It was pitch dark and we could hear the battle raging. Finally, the telephone rang again and the Lieutenant told us we were on a zero alert. Everyone got his gear straightened out and was ready to go. The telephone rang again, and the Lieutenant said,"OK, Sergeant, begin moving the men out."

This was it. We were going to walk right into the enemy's battle. Three men had already gone out the door when the telephone rang again. Everyone froze, and we all stopped to listen. The Lieutenant said, "Yes, uh huh, yes, I see." Finally, he put the phone down and said, "The situation has suddenly changed. You men go try to get some sleep; just don't leave the building." Everyone's breath sounded like a big tire going flat.

Going up to the third floor into a hayloft, I found a discarded sleeping bag, and crawled in. I had dozed off, but was immediately awakened by the earth bouncing up and down, and I thought the building was falling apart around me. I had never heard a bomb hit, but I knew what this was. I unzipped the sleeping bag, jumped up and ran down three flights of stairs, and was in the cellar on my hands and knees trying to dig a hole in the floor with my bare hands before the building stopped shaking.

Anyone who has had a bomb hit close by and has seen what bombs did to the German cities, can't help wondering how in the hell the Germans got through it. It is a wonder they didn't all go nuts, and it is a condemnation of the evil that was Hitler that he would let his people suffer so much.

I talked with a German soldier after the war and he told me about being overjoyed at getting a furlough away from the front and going to his home in Berlin. He said the first evening home he spent all night in ". . . how do you say it, keller?" I said, "You mean cellar." He said, "That is it, cellar — all night I am like the rat, I run this way and that and bombs were falling everywhere." When morning came he said, "To hell with the furlough — let me go back to the front!"

During the next few days, towed-in gliders were dropping supplies, as they silently made their way across our path, while the fighter bombers were busy. The first day I saw a flight of C-47s coming in and suddenly one of them turned nose down, hit the ground, and blew up like a bomb. It was a sickening sight.

I was watching the heavy bombers go over one day and unexpectedly one of them exploded into flames. The ball of fire began falling and about a third of the way to the ground the fire went out, but there was no plane there. The plane and the men had absolutely been blown to bits.

One day when the C-47s were towing in gliders, some of us were watching the show. One of the aircraft got hit by German machine-gun fire, and flames were streaming out from the belly of the plane. It held a true course and the glider did not cut loose until they were at the proper place. Since we were all paratroopers, the first thing that came to our minds was that the crew should bail out. Everyone was yelling "Jump! Jump! Jump!" and I thought the crew was going to wait too long. Just as the glider cut loose, a man came sailing out of the C-47 and his chute opened. In a moment or two another man bailed out. Soon the plane was engulfed in flames and still a third man came through this enormous ball of fire and his chute also opened. We knew there was supposed to be a fourth man in there, probably the pilot, and it looked like he was a goner. Everyone was groaning, when suddenly the plane broke apart and out of that mess of fire and wreckage a dark ball hurtled through the air and a snow white blossom appeared. Someone yelled "Ray!" and everyone was elated. A few days later, I passed the place where the wreckage fell and all that was left was one motor.

Another day, as I watched the P-47s working the Germans over, one of our planes suddenly flipped upside down and, with the motor wide open, it flew about one mile at an altitude of about 150 feet, then hit the side of a big hill, and proceeded to go off like a bomb.

One day during all this activity I was standing by a building in the company of a noncom and an officer. Officers, in general, never gave me much trouble. I left them alone and they left me alone. Every so often, though, you would run into a real rat. These kind of people will use their rank for their own personal gain. The biggest friction I had with the brass was this old Prussian attitude that made it imperative that they treat enlisted men like kids. On the other hand, all through training it is hammered into your head that a good officer always sees to the welfare of his troops. This principle is true in parents, teachers, a foreman — anyone who is in a leadership position. As we stood there, a flight of C-47s came in for resupply. It appeared that they had unloaded too soon and had dropped the supplies on the Germans. Because we were on the other side of the perimeter, I couldn't be sure, because I didn't even know where the lines were over there. The officer said, "The God-damned sons-of-bitches dropped it on the krauts." He shook his fist at the sky. "I hope the krauts shoot every one of the God-damned sons-of-bitches down."

Well, I had been trained in aerial supply and this officer knew better. Every plane in that flight was dropping on the signal of one plane and one man. It could have been a miscalculation, it could have been defective equipment, and it could have been that the man in the lead plane was just shook up and not on the ball. But to bitterly condemn every man up there for one man's mistake was unjustified and a little more than I could stand.

I had heard that this officer was a no-good SOB, but I had not had any personal experience with him previous to this encounter. I was beginning to realize, though, that what I had heard was probably true.

About this time, one of our cooks drove up in a jeep with a big cannister full of hot soup. They used anything they could get their hands on to make this soup. I wouldn't say that it was a gourmet's delight, but it was hot, nourishing, and welcome. The officer rubbed his hands together, grabbed a mess kit, and piled it just as full as he could. He went off toward the door of the building slurping down food as greedily as a pig at the trough. When he was about half-way to the door he turned his head, paused, and as an afterthought said, "Sergeant, see that the men get fed." In a few minutes he had gone from cursing innocent men to their death to happily filling his greedy belly.

Chapter Seven

Odds and Ends

B RIGHT AND EARLY ONE following morning we were moved to a new location. If the brass thought one sector was likely to be hit, they would move us a little closer but still have us in position to move out in any direction. As we headed out across a field we came upon a building by an artillery battery; we realized why we had been moved this way. Several German tanks were scattered across the field and had been knocked out. They had cracked through the lines and had penetrated nearly to our artillery. The artillery boys had depressed their gun tubes and had out shot the Germans with their movable gun turrets. That was real shooting.

These artillery boys were lined up for breakfast, pancakes cooked on a stove just outside the building, and someone in our bunch called out, "Hey, do you all have enough to go around?" One of the artillery boys called back, "Sure, fall in line." We ate, then moved on. I guess those artillery boys were glad to see a little extra infantry ahead of them, especially after what had happened the night before.

We continued across the field until we came to a building that was to be our headquarters for a few days. If I was lucky enough to get guard duty close by, I would sleep in the loft, but sometimes we would catch an outpost in a field. One room in this building was used by a Belgian family as a sitting room and kitchen — a stout, older woman with one eye pointing at two o'clock, a young woman, and a very pretty little girl about two years old. During time off, when we weren't catching a nearby guard post, some of us would congregate in this room. "Mama" would be sewing or peeling vegetables, and the little girl would be sitting on some soldier's knee being stuffed with K-ration chocolate.

"Mama" was a rather cheerful old soul, and she displayed one talent that still amazes me. She couldn't speak a word of English, but she would sit there doing her work with a pleasant half smile on her face. She would be sewing or doing some other chore, the baby would be entertained by some soldier, and we would be horsing around. But if Mama suddenly cocked her head to one side, raising the eyebrow on her good eye, all noise and activity would cease and the room would become completely quiet. If you listened real hard you would hear the low drone of a plane in the distance. If Mama listened for a moment then turned back to her work, everyone would relax and the banter would resume. But if, Mama popped up out of her chair and headed for the cellar, you never saw such a damned stampede. You could put your money on the line that there would be some bombs falling very shortly.

Sometimes, I could hear the aircraft approaching and I could tell the difference between the German and American planes. Because the multi-engined planes of the krauts usually weren't synchronized, they would have a pulsating sound. But Mama could tell the difference between kraut planes and American planes before we could even hear them!

The Germans did most of their bombing on Bastogne, so we really didn't have to worry too much, although the bombs bounced the ground around quite a bit. On the other hand, we never knew when they might go for one of these outlying groups of buildings. One night I got the hell scared out of me. Three of us were sent out in a field to man an outpost. We usually had a "curtain" of these around all Command Posts. Although we weren't in the front lines of fighting at this time, we never knew when the Germans would succeed in breaking through and infiltrating them. It was our duty to take up the slack.

A telephone wire was strung to the outlying post, and the man on watch was almost constantly in contact with the Command Post. If something happened to us on watch and we couldn't be contacted, the Command Post would go on alert.

Our position was by a haystack, and nearby was the tumbled-down remains of a small stable or storage shed, of no value to us as a shelter. A little to the left of this shed we managed to pull out enough hay to cover the snow, assembled our blankets, and lay down to wait out the bitter cold of the night. The man on watch had a good field of vision and laying down with the blanket covering him, made the cold a little more bearable.

We had no more than gotten settled, when the shelling started. For a few minutes that stuff was really falling all round us. One shell came screaming in and hit hard. It was a dud, and for some reason a dud seemed to shake us up more than an explosion. This went on for a few minutes, then all at once the firing was corrected all the way back to some of our artillery positions. This puzzled me. Why did they put those shells out in the middle of that field, then suddenly make a mile correction right on the button? We felt sure that the Germans had spotters within our perimeter, but there was no location close enough to make artillery correction that accurate, and to say it was a miscalculation — well, the krauts weren't that bad at arithmetic.

Nothing happened for a little while, then some German planes came over and began dropping flares. They lit up the countryside almost as bright as day, and it sure gave everyone an eerie feeling. In a few moments some bombs hit back at Bastogne. The planes seemed to be buzzing around up there at a pretty high altitude.

All at once, one of the planes peeled off and went into a power dive, and I knew where that boy was headed. I figured he saw the contrast of the shack and the hay stack, and he thought it was a gun position. I don't know why we didn't get up and run away from the position; we may have thought he would see us and strafe us. Anyway, as he came screaming down out of the night sky the plane got louder and louder, and it seemed as if it was taking forever. While the plane kept coming, I thought that it would surely plunge right into us. Just before it was too late, he pulled out with a mighty swoosh. I swear, I believe his tail dragged the ground as he pulled up. I thought, "Here it comes, this is it!" I drew up in a knot as tight as a fist. But no bomb fell, and in a few moments we realized that he hadn't released one. I thought at the time that in the last moment he saw it wasn't a gun emplacement and was saving his bomb for a better target.

These reprieves from certain death were sure welcome, but I swear they do weary a man.

The rest of the night passed quietly, and at daybreak we gathered up our gear and headed back to the Command Post. But something about that night has always bugged me. How did the artillery come right on top of us, then correct the position one mile — just like that — in one bold stroke; and why didn't the plane drop the bomb? After puzzling over this for several years I think I may have found the solution. We knew there must have been spotters or spies inside our perimeter. Too many coincidences pointed in that direction. Before the snow came, an infiltrator could have sneaked across that tumbled-down mess of boards and debris, dug himself in under some of that junk, and with a supply of food and a radio, he would have been in a great position. This place was off the beaten path, and it would have been purely an accident if he had ever been discovered, especially after the snow came. He could have called in the artillery to try to make us change our position, even if we didn't get hit. It strikes me odd, though, that if this far-fetched solution were so, then when the plane was diving for us, he might well have been frantically whispering into his radio, "Don't drop it, don't drop it!" I have always regretted that I didn't kick around in that mess of junk when morning came. I might have uncovered a rat.

Our planes dropped us galoshes in the air supplies, but our feet were just about gone by then. Our boots and feet had gotten wet the first few days, and when the snow came, the awful cold nearly finished the job. I wiggled my toes all the time, trying to keep my feet from going completely numb and trying to prevent trench foot. The galoshes helped keep our feet drier and a little warmer, but they were heavy and clumsy.

One night I caught a guard post near the Command Post and my feet had been cold so long that I was determined to get them warm at least one time. The stove down in the room never had enough fuel, but I managed to heat some water. When it was hot, I poured it into my helmet, took off my boots, and slid my feet in one at a time. When your feet have been so cold for about ten days — when they feel like they are coming off at the ankles — just to feel them warm for the briefest moment is a great relief. When I finally dried them and tried to put on my boots, I couldn't. My feet were about twice their size, and my guard shift was coming up soon. I finally had to stand my guard in my galoshes. The cold eventually shrank my feet enough that I could get my boots back on, and I never took them off again. But at least one night, for a short time, my feet were warm.

On that Christmas Eve of December 1944, some GIs came by and told us the Germans had set up a loud speaker in front of one of the regimental sectors and were playing "White Christmas." This was the most popular song in the States at that time and the Germans knew it. I wonder if they thought that morale could be broken with that juvenile psychology, or were they feeling the same nostalgia as we were?

Chapter Eight

The Breakthrough

THE DAY AFTER CHRISTMAS, we got word that elements of the Third Army had broken through to us. I believe it was the 4th Armored Division. Of course we were elated, but in a way it was anti-climatic. Before the breakthrough, we had become somewhat mentally conditioned to the fact that we would be there forever. There have been some things said and written about this, but I don't think any of them have ever described it just right. I have searched through the years for the right words, but they still elude me.

If you merely say, "Reinforced," that doesn't do justice to the brilliant operation of the 4th Armored Division and the Third Army in general. If you say, "They helped us," that indicates that they were just side men. On the other hand, if you say, "They rescued us," that indicates we were helpless. Actually, we were in better shape when they broke through to us than we had been since we had arrived. The P-47s had taken a lot of pressure off of us and the air supply had done its part. The feeling that I had about this was that there might be an end to this thing, whereas before the end was nowhere is sight.

The armor coming at the breakthrough was beautiful! And all the crack outfits, including the 101st, were doing a masterful job in carrying out a brilliant plan of teamwork that not only worked, but broke the back of the German armed forces. To repeat a phrase, "The Infantry can't do without the Armor and the Armor can't do without the Infantry." Every man and outfit has it's place, and we would all be in a hell of a shape without the Quartermaster.

The day after the breakthrough, Cappaletti came up to me and said, "Bastogne is swarming with reporters; they're blowing this deal sky high." I stood there in the snow and I was bewildered. I wondered what the reporters were doing there; and then I realized that it had never occurred to me that anyone on the outside had known anything about the situation we were in.

Around this time, the battered old American Eagle seemed to descend on my shoulder, and he gave me a little lesson in greatness. Not that I felt I was great, mind you; hell, I was too scared to be great. But I began to understand the meaning of the word, I think, for the first time in my life. Greatness is not the act, but the attitude while performing the act. If you pursue greatness and happiness, you will probably never find them. They are, rather a by-product of something done for a worthwhile purpose and done unselfishly.

In our ordeal at Bastogne we hadn't fought any harder battles than the rest of the outfits in the Bulge; a battle is a battle, and it takes only one bul-let to kill you. But, because of the situation, we were in a position where our "paper could be graded." It is a little different when you are simply in the lines than when you are surrounded. When you are simply in the lines you can back off a little if things get too hot; but when you are surrounded, you have no place to go. We were aware that we had been handed a very hot potato, yet I had never heard a man gripe about this. I had never heard any man say that he thought we had been thrown a curve. We were all aware that if we held our place, for every mile the Germans failed to advance there would be just that many miles that would not have to be retaken by some poor devils in the attack. Ask any combat man if attacks are not rough.

Brigadier General McAuliffe was supposed to have said when asked how he felt about the rescue, "Again I say nuts. My men are ready to attack."

Later on I ran into a 4th Armored Division boy in the hospital and he told me what the General said and that it hurt his feelings to think that when he was giving everything he had, it was not appreciated. I understood what he meant, but felt that the whole thing was really nothing but a misunderstanding. When the 4th boys broke through to us, we could have turned back flips. The were damned well appreciated, but General Mac was so proud of his boys that even the suggestion that we were helpless was enough to make him act like a setting hen!

I went on to tell him that everybody engaged in this cold bloody thing was doing a real job and that we were well aware of what the 4th Armored was and their reputation, but every man has to have pride in his own outfit — and we were all in it together. I think he understood.

No one at Bastogne who had any view at all of history could keep from equating it with Valley Forge. There is a little difference though. Those old boys at Valley Forge did not have nourishing K-rations, nor did they have air supply. They didn't even have too much backing, but they starved, and froze their feet off, and they damn well succeeded.

I suspect that George Washington never realized that his portrait would be hanging everywhere 200 years later. And I doubt Abe Lincoln knew when he made the Gettysburg Address that it would become a classic. One thing that I do know, though, is that when you are going in the right direction, without trying to capitalize on the notoriety and publicity of your acts, then you just might be doing something that will hold together. Standing in the snow I thought, "Well, hell, you just might have been a tiny part of what makes history without even trying."

We were aware, if we stopped to think about our situation, that we could have never pulled this deal off without the leadership of General McAuliffe. On the other hand, I'm sure he knew that his leadership would have been for nothing if he had not had men that would do their job.

One night, about this time, off to the east I could see V-2s going up into the sky, probably heading for Antwerp. As I watched these rocket missiles, I called them "lousy bastards."

About the time of the breakthrough, Hitler was out there somewhere in his lair, licking his wounds in frustration. Every time that he had tried to steal the egg out of the (American) Eagle's nest, he had gotten a very bloody head. As Hitler realized the futility of his efforts in the Battle of the Bulge, his bitterness increased. In his frustrated anger, he would periodically jump up and throw at us any object at hand — V-2 rocket missiles, you name it, he threw it — but it availed him naught.

There is no doubt in my mind that if they had been willing to pay the price, the Germans could have taken Bastogne. If they had massed all their forces in one place, they may have been able to crack through to Bastogne. But I know, and I think the Germans knew, that if they had chosen that route, the carnage would have been more than even they could stomach.

One morning just at daybreak, my battalion was assembled to go to an undisclosed location. We had gotten some replacements the night before. The platoon that Cappaletti and I were attached to was down to only five men and two noncoms. Two replacements brought our platoon strength up to seven men, and we were very grateful because that meant we would have more men to stand guard at night.

We began moving out about sunup. We were walking on a secondary road that intersected the highway going to Noville. When the battalion had gone far enough so that about two-thirds had turned down the highway toward the town, we suddenly heard a flight of planes. Someone said, "Ah, they're probably ours because it's daylight." I glanced back toward the sound of the aircraft and without a word I dived for the ice. In a few moments all hell broke loose. There was an anti-aircraft machine-gun position nearby that added to the noise. Bombs were falling, machine guns — and I think 20mm cannon from the German planes — were all firing. I was afraid to look up to see if I could better my position, because I feared that even a near miss with a 20mm cannon could ruin my face and eyes. I held my face flat down against the ice with my helmet sheltering my head, expecting to be cut in two any second during the raid, which seemed to last forever.

Finally the pandemonium stopped, and I realized I was still in one piece. I got up and looked about me. There was a bomb crater about 20 or 30 yards to my left, big enough for an automobile. In training films they show the strafing planes plastering the middle of the road, with soldiers scattering to either side. In this case, though, I was surprised that every man lay down in the road, and the German planes worked over the sides. Consequently, not a man in the whole battalion was hit.

When I got up, I knew where I was going. There was a sturdy brick house right against the highway. I was going to this house and if another wave of planes came in, I was going to be on the opposite side of that house. I think Colonel Bob Sink, the Regimental Commander, was "denning" in this house, and evidently he had been watching all the activity from a window. It was about 50 yards from where I had hit the ice to the main highway and the house. I started walking fast, like I knew where I was going. When you do this, no one pays any attention to you. About halfway to the highway, Colonel Sink was facing a scared kid, so scared he was about the color of anemic lard. Accompanying this kid was a Lieutenant. The Colonel addressed the Lieutenant, and as I walked past them I heard the Colonel say, "Lieutenant, can you tell me why this soldier threw his rifle away just because of a little strafing?" I don't think the Colonel cared a damn about the rifle, he was just trying to make the kid mad and in that way the kid would come "unshook."

I walked on until I came to the house and went to the other side, where I could see around the corner and tell when the battalion was ready to move again. Soon a soldier came stepping along toward me. When he got near the corner of the building where I was standing, I asked him, "What the hell are you up to?" and he laughed and said, "The same damn thing that you are." We both laughed as we stood behind the house.

The Colonel was still giving the kid hell for dropping his rifle, but soon he stopped and the battalion began to move. The soldier and I stepped from behind the house and fell into place in line. In combat it never hurts to buy a little extra insurance by playing the percentages.

Walking down the highway, we came to the spot that had been the location of the head of the column during the raid. A young GI was coming toward the rear; he was carrying his helmet by the strap and dragging his rifle by the sling, and he was saying over and over in a bewildered voice, "Somebody tried to lay an egg on me." His face was spattered with mud and I looked to the left and there was a great big bomb crater. He must have split for the side of the road and almost got too far.

On January 5th, 1945, on the front page of *The New York Times,* a picture appeared of my battalion taken just a few minutes after this raid. The picture shows part of the battalion, a bullet-scarred sign saying "Bastogne," some evergreen trees, and the ruins of a building. This was the only authentic war picture, I believe, that was in the little magazine sold in theater lobbies during the showing of the movie "The Battle of the Bulge." You can't tell from the expression on the faces of these men that just beyond the evergreen trees we had been almost frozen in fear as these planes unloaded on us.

We walked down the highway to Noville a good distance, then took a side road that led across a field and into a forest. When we reached our destination, we came upon some holes that had already been dug, and most of them were covered with logs to protect against tree bursts. This area must have been right behind the forward line, and I suppose someone had anticipated an attack here and we had been sent to beef up the lines.

Someone told us to pick a hole and set up shop. Cap and I picked one to our liking and went to work improving it to suit us. We dug a little more and broke small evergreen branches to put in the bottom to keep our blankets from coming in contact with the mud.

Someone had left a bottle of fruit liqueur at this hole, and I tasted it to see if it was any good. It was the best. I told Cap we would save it for nights when we came off guard duty; we could take a little sip and maybe the damned cold wouldn't seem so bad. He agreed that might be a good idea. As we were getting our hole fixed to suit us, a Lieutenant and a Sergeant came up and told us they wanted us to move to another hole. Now combat stress makes a man a little on the edgy side, and I almost blew up on this decision. I said, "I wish the people around here would make up their damned mind." I looked for the Lieutenant to chew me out good, but he didn't say anything, nor did the Sergeant. The incident was soon forgotten.

That night, some of us, including the Sergeant, were standing near our hole eating K-rations and the Sergeant was assigning us our guard watch. Since there were so few of us and our holes were close together, he had figured that one man at a time could stand watch for all the group. He said,"Cap, you stand guard at such an hour, Simms, you get it at another hour; the new men will get it at another hour." Since the new men's hole was a little distance away, I asked the Sergeant, "What about the new men?" He said rather matter-of-factly, "They have a watch."

I asked, "But who is going to wake them up?"

He replied, "Hell, they ain't going to sleep none tonight."

That really tickled my funny bone because of the innocent way that the Sergeant said it, and because I realized that I had become a "veteran." Up

until then I was still thinking of myself as a "greenhorn," and I realized
that I had forgotten that I didn't sleep any the first several nights in combat either. The veteran has more compassion for the novice than the "green
man" ever realizes.

This calls to my mind old "Scared Rabbit." You see anyone knows that
the way to neutralize excess adrenaline is to exercise physically. So when
old "Scared Rabbit" begins to have the adrenaline slopping over the side,
he gets the notion to exercise a little. Now any fool knows that running
toward the rear will get rid of adrenaline twice as fast as running toward
the front, so this is generally the direction "Rabbit" faces when he
scratches off. It seems that he always gets these notions for a little road-
work about the time that everything really heats up. "Rabbit" would probably run halfway around the world if someone didn't snag him as he went
by and say, "Why don't you get the hell back up there where you belong?"

I was sleeping in the hole that night and Cap was standing guard outside. The quick movement of his feet awakened me instantly. About the
same time, he dived into the hole head first and hit a perfect belly buster
right on top of me. I started to say, "What the . . . ," when a covey of
screaming meemies went screeching overhead and landed in back of us.
Instead I said, "It's getting a little sticky out there, isn't it?" Cap had heard
those damned things being fired and knew they were coming our way.

When it was time for me to go on guard, I got out of the hole and Cap
got in. Standing there in the cold eerie silence of the forest, I soon became
aware of a terrible, mysterious roaring somewhere far to the north. It
sounded a great deal like a giant cauldron or kettle bubbling with such
intensity that it kind of worried me. I listened and tried to figure out the
cause. Finally, after several minutes, I began to get the answer. Every
artillery piece in that part of the world — big ones, little ones, far and near
— were all screaming, whooshing, and whistling toward that great roaring
sound. There must have been artillery on the north side of the Bulge that
was also firing on that target. At any rate, from the fast rumbling sound, I
estimated that hundreds of shells per second were landing on the target.
That meant that thousands of shells per hour were hitting the target.

The shelling was going on when I went on guard, and it was still going
two hours later. I don't know how long they ultimately shelled that target,
but I was glad I was not the kraut who had to live through that terrible
barrage. It was one of the most devastating things I ever heard.

The next morning, we were assembled and moved back. The command must have thought the threat of an attack in that area had lessened. We began marching back toward where we had come from. When the head of the battalion column about reached the main highway, we began to run, and I was puzzled because I couldn't understand why we were having to run through the snow with the gear we carried. Running on slick ice and snow and wearing so many clothes and carrying all that gear is difficult.

We ran until the rear of the battalion reached the main highway and then we slowed to a walk. The front of the battalion was quite a way down the highway toward Bastogne.

As we got out on the highway, here came the artillery shells screaming, busting out all over the place. As I dived for the hard slick ice I thought, "Now I know why we've been running. The krauts have this road intersection zeroed in and those devils up front ran till they got out of the zero area. Now they are tired and are lying down to rest, while we're stuck right on target."

During the interval when the Germans were reloading, I looked around and both the new boys had been slightly wounded, enough to be evacuated. Our new help had lasted about 24 hours. I decided the best thing to do was get up and move away from this intersection. I had hurt my back the day before when I had hit the ice during the strafing raid, and it was still pretty sore and stiff. Now as I slipped and slid on the ice to get a foothold to get up, my back hung up in one of those catches that only bad backs can have and I couldn't stand. I was floundering and rolling over but every time I tried to rise it felt as though I was being stabbed by a red hot poker. Finally, I managed to get in position so that I was gradually able to get on my feet. A Sergeant who was behind at the tail end of the battalion came walking up, and I said, "Sergeant, I have hurt my back and when I get down I can't get up, so I'm not going to lie down again, and I'm not going to stand here in this zeroed area." He said, "I'm with you — let's go." I could tell from his voice that he had sized up our situation, and it seemed to have teed him off a bit. As we began moving toward the front direction somebody yelled, "Don't crowd up!" The Sergeant snarled back, "If you don't want us to crowd up you get up off your dead ends and get moving."

Finally, after we walked almost to the middle of the column, we were out from under the artillery and the battalion got up and began to move. We were some distance from where we were going, and carrying this load and having run that distance, the sweat was really beginning to pour. When we finally arrived at our destination, I just pitched my gear in a barn and went outside in the cold to try to cool off. Of course, then the old wet underwear felt cold and uncomfortable again.

Later that afternoon, I was walking through a barnyard and feeling pretty stoved up from my hurting back and all that sweating and cooling with wet underwear. I was about as stiff as a horse ridden hard and put away wet, and my spine felt like a broom handle with arthritis.

I saw Vernon Agy facing the Lieutenant, and the Lieutenant was speaking to him in a very animated manner. By the time I got to them, they both turned and went off in different directions, so I walked up to a soldier who had been standing nearby and asked him, "What gives?" He said that Agy had heard that a wall had been blown out of a wine cellar back at Bastogne and he had been trying to borrow a jeep to go get some. The Lieutenant heard about this plan and had given Agy orders not to do this. Of course, the Lieutenant hadn't gotten out of sight before Agy conned some artillery officer out of a jeep and he went back to Bastogne, got a bunch of wine, and brought it back. Agy was a master scrounger. He always tried to get enough for everyone to share. Along about dark, the men began dropping into the room where Agy had set up his display. Some took a drink or two and left; I think Cap only took a little and was in and out, but about eight or ten of us old saltheads got down to real business. The people who lived there had withdrawn to other rooms, so we had this room all to ourselves.

As the alcohol began to warm up our old bones, we began to swap information about what had happened to the guys that were no longer with us. Quite a few faces were missing, and it seemed that a lot of them were new men. Someone told about one soldier who had previous combat experience, who got hit in the hand when we were up at Noville. Now a hand wound can be extremely painful, and this boy in his misery begged some of his buddies to kill him. Of course they refused, because they knew the medics would soon get to him and give him morphine. As this was all going on, a shell came in and killed him.

Someone told about one of the veterans being teamed up with a green, nervous-type kid as we were going into Noville. When all the lead and hell broke loose, this nervous kid said that he was not about to go in there. He was supposed to have said, "Hell, no, I'm not going in there — that's too rough for me!" Well, this "seasoned" soldier comes out with a P38 kraut pistol and he puts it up to this kid's head and says, "Hell, yes, you're going in there. I'm going in there and you're going with me." The kid went, of course.

The next day, when we were beginning to withdraw from Noville, Agy said that he and Hanson and one of the "nervous" kids were lying behind a haystack on the northern outskirts of the town. A German shell came in, hit the top of the haystack, and exploded hay all over the place. In a few minutes another shell came in and took about half of what was left of the stack. Agy said he turned to Hanson and said, "I believe it's about time to go." He said they looked around, and that scared kid was already 50 yards away, looking back and running scared. You see the kid wouldn't leave without permission, but when Agy said it was time to go that was all he needed.

As we warmed to the task of dispensing with the wine everyone began to get more humorous and tried to put the tragic events aside. Agy and Hanson were sitting on the floor, leaning back against the wall on one side of the room. I was standing opposite them at the other side of the room. The other guys were sprawled all over the room. Suddenly Agy cocked one eyebrow up, and with his long hair hanging over one eye and a crooked grin on his face he said, "Simms, can't you just see your folks turning through the Sears Roebuck catalog trying to figure out how to spend your insurance money?"

I said, "Hell! Man don't talk like that!" and I knew as soon as I said it that I had done played right into Agy's trap because all the men just roared with laughter. I had learned a long time earlier that if you were being teased that if you can't whip them you better join them. The men began to milk the mental image. One fellow said, in a high feminine voice, "Oh, I've been wanting a fur coat like that." All the time he would go through the motions of leafing through a catalog. Another guy pretended to leaf through the catalog, and he said in a deep voice, "I've been wanting me a shotgun like that and now I've got the money to get it." This went on for about 15 minutes, and the only way I saw to get off the hook was to pretend to be real shook up. I must have done a convincing job because they laughed until tears came to their eyes.

About this time one of these old knuckleheads reminded us that we would be alerted to go back in the lines, probably the next day or that next night. Word was that German artillery in that sector was "just plain hell," he added. He then went on to say, "I suggest we sing a song appropriate for the occasion; let's sing "Lord, I'm Coming Home."

That took me back a bit, and I said, "Maybe we'd better not sing that," but he replied, "Well, hell, it's so, ain't it?"

So, we began singing, off-key harmony. After a verse or two, it became right pretty. Everyone seemed to become lost in his own thoughts, though we all knew we were thinking about how many had already gone, who would be next, would it ever be over, or were we just doomed to war forever or death. We seemed to be saying "Old Man Death, I know you want me, and you may get me, but you'll never break me." I believe it was about the strangest thing I've ever experienced.

We had gone through the song about five times, when the door burst open and in stepped the Lieutenant. I just about dropped my teeth. After the Lieutenant had ordered Agy *not* to get the wine, there we were caught red-handed, and I could just see a court-martial or being shot at sunrise. I was holding a bottle in my right hand, but before the Lieutenant could get his eyes adjusted, I eased it down behind me and set it on a table. Agy was sitting across the room and before the Lieutenant could speak, Agy held up his bottle and in a jolly good mood said, "How about a drink, Lieutenant?"

To everyone's surprise, the Lieutenant took the bottle from Agy and proceeded to take a long swallow. When he had enough he handed the bottle back to Agy, wiped the back of his hand across his mouth, and said, "That's pretty good stuff, Agy." Agy casually said, "Oh, we always try to keep the best."

The Lieutenant stood around for a bit, chatting as friendly as could be, and making no mention of the wine. Frankly, I couldn't figure this out, but I was glad that we seemed to be off the hook.

Finally the Lieutenant said, "Well, I better be going, you men be careful," and as he closed the door behind him, and when I was sure he was out of earshot, I turned toward Agy with frank admiration and awe, and exclaimed, "You low-down SOB, you got away with it." Old Agy slapped his leg, and shook his head from side to side as he laughed.

Agy was at his best when he played and won these little games with the lesser brass. He was especially pleased when he won, and when he knew the lesser brass knew he had won. I always believed he had a secret ambition to put some Captain or Lieutenant in a Section 8. After all, what is a

Lieutenant to do, put all his men in the jug and go off and fight the battle alone? Not on your life, and old Agy pretty well had this figured, and that is why he thought he could get away with it.

I stayed with the party until about midnight. Everyone was ready to turn in so I left, walked through the snow around to the other side of the building, and climbed a ladder to a third story hayloft in the barn part of the building and went to sleep.

About 2 a.m. I woke up freezing, and my head felt as though a meat cleaver was resting right between my ears. I thought about the party and wondered if it had been worth it. I climbed down to a space just inside the door. I was stamping my feet and smoking a cigarette when a field grade officer came lumbering out of the hay and headed outside in search of a "fire plug." When he saw me standing just inside the outer door, he came awake and climbed on my back. "If you're on guard, why aren't you outside where you can see?"

Well, I was about half ill from the aftermath of that party, so just as belligerent as I thought I could get away with I replied, "Sir, I'm not on guard. I'm just down here because I got so cold!" He didn't buy that so we argued about it a bit, then he went on outside. I decided if I went away while he was out there he would really think I was putting him on, so I waited until he came back in. He walked past me without a word, went back in the hay, and I could hear him grumbling and otherwise raising hell with a Sergeant because there wasn't any guard out there. When I heard this I scooted up the ladder and climbed under the hay; they couldn't have found me with a bloodhound.

The next night we assembled after dark and then moved out. We didn't know who we were going to relieve, but figured it would be one of the battalions in our own regiment, the 506th. Our group walked along in the snow for some time and finally we came to a forested area. The road we were on went through this area of woods, intersecting with another road running along in front of the trees. Just inside the edge of the trees were our lines, along the right side of the road. The woods on the left dropped back sharply to the rear for about 75 yards, and our lines were just on the edge of these woods. The road we had entered went straight ahead for about a quarter mile and entered another wooded area. The road that ran parallel to the woods we were in continued across a field to our left. The Germans were supposed to be in the woods in front of us.

As soon as our group got to the lines, noncoms and officers began taking us in tow and dropping us off in the lines at the places they wanted us to be.

A Sergeant took myself and Cappaletti and started down the line to the right of the road. Just inside the edge of the wood next to the road, there was a path. The snow had been packed down on it until it was brick hard and as slick as glass. The men who had occupied this sector had dug their holes on either side of this path, which was left open so that they could easily move up and down the front. The Sergeant could drop a rifleman off in almost any hole, but since Cap and I had the bazooka, he wanted us in just the right place.

He started to put us in a hole right next to an artillery forward observer, but there were too many low-hanging limbs. You want an open field of fire when you shoot that thing, because if you want to keep breathing for the next few minutes, you don't want the shell to hit anything as it leaves the tube.

We began moving on down the line, and for some reason I was walking in front of Cap and the Sergeant. Without warning, the world suddenly fell away from me and I was going, going, gone. Although the holes we had seen had been dug on either side of the path, some joker had dug his right in the path. It was dark in that thick evergreen forest, and I had stepped into a large hole. As I fell, the corner of my forehead hit the frozen rim on the side of the hole and somehow the shin of my leg cracked the edge of the hole on the other side. After falling about six feet, I hit the bottom with a thud. My shin and my head hurt so bad I couldn't even holler. I just lay there gritting my teeth, wondering if the pain would ever stop. Cap knelt down by the hole and frantically asked if I was all right? I hurt too bad to answer, and he again called to me. He was about to get down in the hole, but I managed to say, "Yes, Cap, I'm all right." As soon as the pain subsided a bit, I thought how stupid war is and how little sense people have to think they can gain from war — and especially I thought about what a vulture Hitler was to cause all this misery in the world. I also thought how good it would be to be away from this cold, desolate, brutal place and be somewhere warm, comfortable, and safe.

I also thought of something else. I thought about how stupid it was for some guy to dig this elephant trap right in the path when everyone else had the good sense to dig theirs on either side. As I pondered about this, my dutiful apathy was replaced by good old Scotch-Irish temper. I hope nothing ever happened to the guy who dug that hole, because as long as he is alive and healthy, I will always remember the soliloquy of expletives that I delivered as being my masterpiece. I wouldn't feel right saying bad things about someone who had had bad luck. That was the deepest damned hole I ever saw. The guy that dug it couldn't even fire from it without standing on a footstool or something. You could stay in there a week and be eligible to join the miner's union. I couldn't even get out of the damned thing. The Sergeant and Cap waited patiently until I gathered myself together, then they both hauled me up to the surface again.

We started on down the path again and I was very careful to let the Sergeant go in front this time — let *him* fall in the next bear trap! We finally turned around and started back toward the road and I was very cautious when we went by that hole, shying away from it like a nervous goat from an electric fence. When we got back out to the road, Cap noticed blood running down my face. He said to the Sergeant, "Look here, Sergeant, doesn't he need to go to the medic?" and the Sergeant said, "It wouldn't be a bad idea." But I insisted that I was all right, and soon the Sergeant found the hole that he thought would be best for us.

Our hole was located on the angle where the roads intersected and because of the arrangement of the terrain, we were out in the open, ten yards in front of the right side of our lines and 75 yards in front of the left side. There were enough bare hardwood trees bordering the road to cause tree bursts if they were hit. We were also in a position to be directly observed by the Germans. But we were put there because this position faced directly down the road that entered the other woods, about a quarter mile away. If an attack came, we would be in a position to use the bazooka — if we lived that long. In order for us to protect this position as long as possible in an attack, we were assigned a rifleman who might be able to pick some kraut off before we were picked off. Because it was dark, it was hard to become oriented to all the relative positions, but we were told that the road was mined at the point where it entered the gate that went into the other woods.

Our new hole was not a very good one, but we bedded down to split the watch and to sleep, with the night passing uneventfully except for the usual shelling. If you don't get knocked off by a shell almost three or four times a night, it is considered quiet. The usual, persistent, and terrible cold was forever with us, compressing us into a numbing miserable state of existence. One thing that made the dread of being hit so bad was the fact that the cold made you feel that it would hurt so bitterly.

Morning came, and Cap and I went to work on that hole. We had to work in plain sight of the Germans, if he wanted to see, but we were determined to make the hole safer and warmer. I half expected a sniper to open up on us but none ever did. There were no logs or poles available to cover our hole, but we found enough broken branches to weave a roof to hold a little dirt, and we soon had a covering about eight inches thick. This would be enough to give us some protection from tree-burst fragments. We left one end of the hole uncovered; this would be where we would fire from and also where the night guard would stand. The men sleeping would be back under the cover. If a shell came in too close, the man on guard could momentarily duck under the cover.

The rifleman who had been assigned to us was a pretty good kid, about 18 years old, but a little on the brash or flippant side. This didn't bother me any because I had worked with kids; however, it caused a little personality conflict between Cap and the kid. Cap and I had never discussed it, but we both believed in trying to stay alive. We were aware that we had to do what we must, but there was no reward in being stupid. So, I had perfect confidence that Cap wouldn't do anything foolish that might get us killed, and he had perfect confidence that I wouldn't either.

This kid, however, seemed to have plenty of nerve — maybe too much. If Cap would caution him about being too careless about exposing himself, he more than likely would give Cap a sassy answer. This irritated Cap, but didn't really amount to much because tempers are always edgy in the lines. During the day Cap or I stayed by the hole at all times, but at daybreak, this kid would go off rambling around and might not come back till night. If one of us wanted to go back into the cover of the woods to shoot the bull with others back there, or to stretch our legs and loosen up, the one going back would quickly get in the cover of the woods while the other stayed at the hole.

One day, about one o'clock, the kid came walking down the road that went across the field to our left. He was strutting along as if he were going down "Main Street," and a sniper could have picked him off like shooting a fish in a barrel. If you have to go out in the open in No Man's Land for a reason, that's one thing, but to go out there when you don't have to is foolhardy. When the kid came up to the hole, Cap admonished him about this. The kid flippantly replied, "That's what I've been trying to do, get shot in the leg and then I could get out of this damned place." Well, that burned Cap, and I thought I was going to have to separate them.

The most unbearable thing we had to contend with was the cold. Twenty-four hours a day you'd wiggle your toes to try to keep the circulation in your feet. We had the unhappy experience of feeling nothing but extreme misery that bordered on pure torture. The nights were the worst and when it was your turn for guard, that was the worst of all. When you had to get up out of the miserable cold hole, the true suffering began. When you stand guard outside, in that cold, by yourself and try to guess when you've been up for two hours, that even makes it worse. After five minutes you start thinking, "Well, I've been up five minutes, only one hour and fifty-five minutes left to go." You try not to dwell on it, but your mind comes right back to it. After 15 or 20 minutes you began to lose your judgment of time, and by then you are so cold you wonder how you are going to stand it for another hour and a half. Finally, after thinking of everything to take your mind off the cold, you conclude that an hour has passed. Now, all there is to look forward to is another hour more miserable than the first.

At intervals a flare would be shot up, and while it was suspended up there by its little parachute, the world would be bright and seemingly warmer and more friendly. And while you had the light, you really gave the terrain at the front a real eyeballing. Finally, the flare would descend slowly to earth and go out, and your little world would be plunged back into a cold ghostly gloom, almost worse than before.

After we had been there a day or two, it began to snow again, and this was a real corker. Snow came down for about 36 hours! Cap and I staked the end of a shelter-half down to the ground and put poles under the other end so that the man on guard could stand in the open end of the hole and see out while he had a little cover from the snow. With the snow whirling silently down on an already white world, visibility was cut virtually to zero. When the flares would go off, you couldn't see them, but the falling snow was eerily illuminated.

One night during the snowstorm, a Lieutenant came down to our hole shortly after dark. He had a bottle of brandy with him and said he figured that if each man took only one good swallow, there would be enough to go around. "I'm sorry," he added, "I don't have any more; but maybe this will help a little." I think every man would have choked before he would have taken any more than his share. There wasn't enough to do much good, though the hot burning liquid in the throat seemed to help a little. It was the thought that did the most good. The Lieutenant could have kept it all for himself and we wouldn't have known the difference.

Another night, while I was sleeping, Cap tapped my boot to tell me it was time for me to go on. It's a peculiar thing, but I could tell time better when I was asleep than I could when I was awake. In light combat sleep there is a little time clock that keeps ticking, unbothered by all the distractions of war. I knew what the matter with Cap was, though. The cold was getting to him tonight. I'm sure that I shorted him some nights for the same reason, but he never complained, so I got up to take my shift. Some nights the cold got to you worse than others and then guard duty was real bad. Other nights you had more strength and toughness, and on those nights you would try to give your partner extra good measure. If you sensed a weakening of your partner, you seemed to gather extra strength to compensate. One thing you didn't want to do and that was cheat your buddy. A strange sense of comradeship and loyalty grows between combat men.

An officer one evening came to our hole and told us that a two-man patrol would check out by our hole and would also check back in with us. We got the password and countersign down pat, and after about an hour the two men came down to the lines to check out. They told us approximately where they were going and how long they expected to be gone. We rechecked the password and countersign and quizzed them briefly about their mission so that there would be no foul-up when they came back toward our lines. They were going about five-eighths of a mile, until they were in the woods to the front, then they were to turn right on a wooded road and go another quarter mile or more; then they were to return by the same route and check back in. The area on that side road was where everyone seemed to think the Germans would be.

They left and I expected them to be gone the better part of an hour. To my amazement, in about 20 minutes I saw two dark figures coming toward me out of the gloom and from the direction in which they had gone. I knew it was too soon for them to be back, and if these figures were Germans, how had they avoided the patrol? I picked up a grenade and got a firm grip on the ring. I let them approach to within ten yards of the hole, then I challenged them. They answered, but it was too low and mumbling for me to understand, so I challenged with the password again, and I still couldn't understand what they said; but I had been studying them all the while and I was sure they were the two men that had gone out, so I told them to come on up. They came up to the hole and squatted down. I said, "You sure got back in a hurry. I didn't expect you so soon, and I couldn't understand your countersign, and if you had made one false move you were about to get this grenade." They mumbled something noncommittal and then asked if we had room enough for them in our hole. I told them I was sorry but we barely had room for ourselves. They said they had to kill about 15 minutes. Of course I knew why they gave the countersign so low. They wanted to get back in without anybody except us knowing it. I also knew why they were back so soon. They had walked over to that gate, stood around a little, agreed on a decision, and had come straight back. The funny part is I didn't blame them. They had been handed a loaded deck and they knew it, and I knew it. The fresh snow was two feet deep and with no broken trails. If the Germans had an outpost over there on that side road, they would have been able to see these men like a sore thumb sticking up in a lotion advertisement. With their dark uniforms, floundering along in that deep snow, the krauts could have cut the men down without warning. The kraut holes had been snowed over and camouflaged so well that if the men had seen the krauts, it would have been their death warrants. They squatted by the hole for 15 or 20 minutes, then got up and went on back to make, what I am sure was an astonishingly accurate report.

One morning we prepared to move up. The other outfits in this area of the Bulge had been hammering away by straightening or flattening out this circle that had been the perimeter around Bastogne. Since we were located on the north of the circle, we had been in a "wait and see" attitude, but now it was time to start the push that would begin squeezing the Bulge together.

Another battalion was to go through our lines and lead the way. We were told to hold our position until they reached their objective, then we were to leave our position and move in behind them. In case the Germans should counter-attack, we would then be in a position to beef up the lead battalion. We were certain that the krauts were no longer interested in Bastogne, but for tactical reasons, to facilitate getting all the men and equipment out of the Bulge, they might want to repossess some strategic position.

As we waited, a jeep came across the field to our left with two recon men. They stopped at the crossroads and engaged us in conversation to find out all we knew about the situation at the front. We told them where we thought the krauts might be, and I told them the road ahead was mined just as it entered the gate about a quarter mile to the front of us. They drove off toward the mined area. The snow was deep and I didn't hear any mines go off. But there might have been a reason for this because at the same time they drove off, our artillery began. The only thing wrong was that it was falling on us. Then when our artillery started, the krauts figured this was an attack, so they started throwing in their artillery, For about a minute or two we were getting it from two sides. There was a forward observer for the artillery up there and he soon got ours corrected. During this time of exploding shells, the recon men must have hit the mines, because when the real move up began, these recon men came back by our hole, on stretchers.

As this battalion came through our lines to make the advance, I recognized two or three Lieutenants from an earlier encounter. I was somewhat reticent to yell out at them so I just played it cool. When each of these Lieutenants came abreast of our hole, they each recognized me. "Hey, Simms, glad to see you, boy, good to see you're OK." It's always good to see that someone you know has made it.

As the men filed past, the tanks began to move up, and before long a soldier came walking to the rear with about a dozen prisoners. One of them had been shot in the leg, and he was being supported by two other men. The krauts had lost much of the aggressiveness they had shown in the early days of the Bulge. As we waited, someone passed the word that the 501st Regiment had reached its objective, and about this time our 506th was reaching its objective. There were a few stray bullets ricocheting through the trees above us, but the action seemed to be relatively light. Soon after the other battalion had entered the woods to the front, we were called out of the lines and assembled to move up.

We walked to the front until we entered a gate. There sat the jeep that had carried the first recon men. The front end looked as if it had been pushed into a smelter. I wondered why men, recon or no, would drive over mines that they knew were there.

As we began to enter the woods, we got a pretty good swarm of artillery fire, and some of it was mighty close. But we kept going until we came to a road that went to the right. We turned right and started down the road. After about 200 yards, I noticed a big stack of cord wood just off the road.

Just as I spotted this it, Cap turned his head and said, "Simms, do you see what I see?" I replied, "I know what we will cover our hole with tonight."

We walked on until we were about 200 yards past this stack of cord wood, then we were stopped and we just stood around for the rest of the day. There seemed to be some indecision as to what was going to happen and what was to be expected. Had we dug in during daylight, we could have gone back to the stack of wood and gotten enough logs to cover our hole, but as it was after dark before we were told to dig in, that altered our plans. We were outside in the snow until nightfall, at which time we ate a cold K-ration. Finally, about 7 or 8 o'clock, we were told to dig in for the night.

Chapter Nine

Night of Hell

WHEN WE WERE FINALLY given the order to dig in, it was too dark and too far to go stumbling back through the snow for the logs. When you are in a wooded area, the cover over a hole is real important. Shells coming in with instantaneous fuses will explode when they hit any limb large or small. When these shells burst up in a tree they spray down into the hole. Now a ground burst can't hurt you in a hole unless it is a direct hit. And high-explosive shells with instantaneous fuses can hit a hole covered with eight-inch logs and still give you a chance to survive.

The three of us: Cap, the kid, and I began to dig. We had only entrenching shovels, so we took turns in the hole. The kid worked willingly enough, and we made good progress. Sometimes, though, it seems foolish to dig when there is no artillery coming in. Since there were three of us, we had to dig a pretty large hole, and along toward midnight we had a fairly decent hole in the making. Suddenly the kid said, "You guys can dig all night if you want to, but I'm going to bed." He didn't know it, but that statement sealed his doom. Cap and I were busy breaking branches to cover the hole to help keep out the cold. We didn't even answer him, so he got in the hole and went to sleep. We kept breaking branches and placing them over the hole, until finally Cap said, "Simms, whatcha say we call it a night?" I replied, "You go ahead and get in the hole, Cap. I want to get just a few more of these branches." You see, Cap and I did everything by mutual consent. If I had asked him to stay up and help me he would have done so without a word of disagreement, but since we had done all we could do, I agreed that he should get in the hole and let me do just a little more to my satisfaction. It turned out that that was the wisest thing I ever said, and I will remember my decision until my dying day. I had no inkling of what this little conversation would mean, but I was soon to find out.

The kid got in the hole first, and he instinctively picked the least dangerous spot. In a large hole the best place is on the side next to the enemy because any spray of shell fragments will have a tendency to spray over your position. Now this kid wasn't scared. If anything, he wasn't scared enough, and if you called his hand in picking the best place he would have exchanged willingly. Cap got in the hole, and for several minutes I broke branches and placed them over the hole. When I saw it was useless to try to improve it anymore, I slid down into the end of the hole and prepared to get some shuteye. Since the kid had already picked his spot on the side next to the krauts, it was only natural for Cap to pick the middle position, so when I got into the hole I was on the side away from the krauts.

As I eased down into position, I found there wasn't enough room for me to lie on my back as was my custom. I could have pushed and shoved until I got enough room, instead I lay down on my left side and promptly went to sleep.

The circumstances and coincidences of this night were to become almost unbelievable. If anything that happened had been changed just a bit in timing, I would not be writing this today.

I had been asleep about an hour and it was close to one o'clock when I was awakened by the heaviest artillery barrage that I had ever been under. The shells were coming in great numbers and they were hitting extremely close. Although a great many were striking very near our position, they seemed to be equally distributed all over this wooded area. As I lay there I thought that when the krauts withdrew from this position they made sure they had this place zeroed in; and now that everyone was bedded down, they were pouring on the coal.

I was scared, and hoped it was only harassing fire and soon would lighten up a bit. I was wrong. Suddenly the world exploded. The blast was felt more than heard, and something like a giant sledge hammer struck me on the shoulder. Cap and I simultaneously gave out with that involuntary yelp that is particular to men being hit by large shell fragments. It goes something like "Ow — oh —." I hurt so bad I couldn't say anything after the first yelp, but Cap was calling for a medic. I heard someone answer, so I told Cap to take it easy because they had heard him. He stopped calling and we lay quietly for a few minutes. Suddenly he said, "Listen to him, here we are maybe dying and he hasn't even woken up; he's snoring his head off." I had heard the same sounds and I knew different. And I realized that Cap and I were both slightly addled by the concussion of that shell. Cap seemed to be more excitable than usual, and my speech had become deliberate and measured, and I seemed to have no control over this condition. I had to make a decision on what to say to Cap about the kid's snoring. I was reluctant to tell him the truth because I was afraid it would scare him, but I figured he would realize the situation pretty soon anyway.

"He's not snoring, Cap; he's dying."

At this, Cap spiritedly disagreed and he replied, "I know he's just sleeping; listen to him snore."

The kid must have been hit in the head and the chest because he never made a sound except for the gurgling in his throat; it was obvious that he was a goner. For Cap and me to argue about whether the kid was asleep or dying wasn't going to do any of us any good, so I said, "Look, I'll show you." My upper right arm and shoulder were useless, but I had some control over my lower arm and hand. Since I was already lying on my left side facing Cap, I leaned against him as far as I could, worked my right lower arm across his body and took hold of the boy's arm. I shook it and called him by name. Of course there was no response.

We lay still for a few moments and tried to take stock of the situation. Cap asked me how bad I was hit and I said, "I'm hit pretty bad in the shoulder but I think I will be all right. I asked him where he was hit and he said, "I'm bleeding bad, Simms." I asked him where he was bleeding, and he said he was bleeding from the area of his kidney. That meant that a slug had gone entirely through him and if it had severed a big blood vessel, then he needed help and in a hurry.

I didn't tell him that he was in grave danger; he already knew that. I decided to try to do something that might help as a stopgap. I couldn't raise myself to a sitting position because I had no leverage in my neck, shoulder, or back and the branches covering our hole prevented me lunging to a sitting position. I thought that if I could only get in a kneeling position I might be able to call someone and make sure I directed him to our hole. If there was an interval in the shelling I might be able to use my good arm and hand to use some of his clothes to press against his wound until help arrived.

I bunched my left arm under me and gave a mighty lunge at the same time as I shoved up, jerked my left hand up and tried to grab the brush. If I could just get hold of it with my good hand, I might be able to work my head up through it, get on my knees, and then use my good hand to throw the brush off and have room to work. As long as I was in a lying position I couldn't get my good hand to Cap's wound. Every time I made this lunge to grab the brush and sit up, my head would hit the brush first and cause me to miss with my hand. When I missed, I would fall heavily back to the bottom of the hole. I had repeated this procedure about four or five times when, without warning, it hit. I went into shock.

Shock is not recognized by untrained people. When it's caused by bleeding, there simply isn't enough blood for the heart to pump. When it's caused by a serious and painful wound without bleeding, the body and nervous system, in trying to cope with this, sometimes get confused and don't function normally. There seems to be a sudden relaxation of blood vessels in the abdomen, hence a sudden drop in blood pressure. The heart is like a pump that has lost its prime. There is still the same amount of blood to try to fill up twice as much plumbing. As the vital organs call for blood, the heart may speed up to try to supply it, but without enough blood to pump, the heart itself may begin to starve. This can be a very dangerous condition for a person who is badly hurt. Fortunately for me, I had a little training along this line, so I recognized the situation the instant it hit me.

On the last lunge that I made trying to sit up, the pain struck. I felt as if someone had taken a sledge hammer and swung it with all his might and hit me in the abdomen. The pain was awful, but then it turned into a burning, searing pain. My whole abdominal cavity felt as though it had been filled with a red hot burning liquid under unbearable pressure. At the same time, a sinking nauseous feeling swept over me, and the world turned into a spinning black void that gave me a feeling of total helplessness and disorientation.

I knew that our lives might depend on my retaining consciousness because if I passed out, Cap would soon go into a coma, and then in all the confusion of this artillery bombardment we might be overlooked and ultimately die in this God-forsaken hole. I flipped my helmet up so that my head would go a little lower, hooked my heels up over the top of the hole, and had my leg and abdominal muscles tensed by the time I was in this upside-down position. My desire for air was insatiable, but to breathe too fast in this situation will black you out even quicker, so I would take about two shallow breaths and then tense my abdominal and leg muscles with all my might, trying to force a little more blood to my heart and head. The world was still spinning in a dark void, but remarkably I retained my thinking. To clamp my abdominal muscles against that red hot sausage grinder in my belly was torture, but if I was to retain consciousness I must. It was such a terrible ordeal that I was tempted to just give up and mercifully pass out, but I knew if I did I might die, and above all, I think knowing that I might be Cap's only link to life was what kept me going and gave me strength.

I would take two short breaths, then clamp down on my stomach muscles, holding my breath and squeezing for about ten seconds; then I would relax for a moment, take a couple of little gulps of air, and repeat the process. I kept at this for several minutes, although it seemed like a lifetime. Finally, the awful pain in my abdomen began to subside a little and the whirling began to stabilize. I knew I had won the battle, so I gave one more tremendous squeeze on my muscles and lay back exhausted with sweat dripping from my forehead.

I was so wrung out that for several moments I couldn't do anything. In a few moments someone came up to the hole, squatted down, and told us that a medic would be there shortly. I told him if he would clear the brush off the hole and help me out, then the medic could get in there with Cap. Reaching in the hole and with shear perseverance he helped me get out. Do you know who it was? You guessed it; another of those damned scrawny kids. It seemed as if I was always running into kids that should be weaker than me, but I was always getting strength from them. I think this was the same little devil that kept me from giving in that night I was so cold.

When I got out of the hole, the first thing I did was look at the hardwood bush on the opposite side of me. I figured that the shell had hit one of its limbs and exploded, but the bush showed no sign of having been hit. This left one alternative, the shell had hit the brush on the hole. I figured that I had had an artillery shell go off about two feet away and I was walking away from it! If the shell had hit the bush, then the slug would have hit me at an angle. The slug that hit me had been traveling straight down. No air bursts were hitting here; it was all ground burst or tree burst. And there were no trees close enough to cause this.

There was a slight lull in the shelling just as I got out of the hole, then it began again in terrible fury. A medic came up and I told him where Cap was wounded so that he could help him without delay. He got into the hole and began to give Cap first aid immediately.

The shelling had reached a high intensity and I was standing exposed with no place to go. Shells were bursting on all sides, some so close they were deafening. Occasionally I could hear a shell fragment spending itself in the dark with a dull but deadly buzz. I had the disquieting thought that if by coincidence my hole was directly zeroed in by one of these cannons, any shell it fired would hit very close to me. Since there was no place to go and no place to seek protection, all I could do was just stand there and take it. In order to play the percentages to the end, I did the only thing available to me. I carefully worked myself down on my knees, then I sat back on my feet, and using my good hand to brace myself, I leaned down as far as I could. This way I figured I would offer a lower target.

I saw that the medic had turned Cap on his side, and I saw him applying a big white bandage. I felt somewhat relieved because I knew Cap was getting help from the people who had the best chance to save him.

In the meantime, the shelling was so bad I expected to get a fatal hit any moment. When a man's tour of combat duty is about over, it is a known fact that in the last few days he really sweats. When you have been knocked out of the war with a big steel slug and the only thing between you and safety is evacuation, and in this situation you're caught exposed in the middle of a deadly artillery barrage, that stuff coming out of your skin isn't sweat. This went on for about 15 minutes and it was a nightmare.

Another medic came down a little slope from the road and squatted by the hole. He and the other medic tending Cap talked for several minutes. They seemed oblivious to this rain of hell. Finally, he came over to me and asked if I could walk. I struggled to my feet and told him that I could, but that I couldn't get up by myself if I lay down. He said, "Well, you come on with me."

I asked, "What about Cap?"

He said, "He'll have to go on a stretcher; I'm going to start evacuating everything that can walk or crawl and get all the casualties out that I can, and maybe this stuff will quiet down directly and we can get out the stretcher cases. We are going to be carrying men out of here all night."

This made sense to me, so I followed him up the hill to the road. When we got up onto the road, there was a jeep and in the back seat were two or three other wounded men. The medic got in the driver's seat and I gingerly eased myself into the passenger side. He was about to start off when he saw another man lying just to his left.

Just as he started to get out of the jeep, a big man came lurching out of the woods, grabbed the side of the jeep and in a pitiful whisper said, "Somebody please help me; I'm bleeding to death!" The medic told him "OK," just as soon as he could get this fellow in they would be going back and the man could be helped at the aid station. Although it's crucial to help a bleeder at once, the help is of much greater value if there is light and plasma.

When he got out of the jeep to help this other fellow, I felt very vulnerable sitting up high and totally exposed to the shelling, so I got out on my side, which was the side toward the Germans. The medic seemed to be taking longer than I anticipated, and now I was feeling uneasy with the delay. I called to the medic that I was going to stand by the tank, just off the road, some 15 yards away and asked him to yell when he was ready. But after moving only about five yards, I heard a shell coming in and in my addled condition I turned toward it and followed the sound with my eyes until it came right in and exploded right in front of me at a distance of about five yards. It never touched me, but the jeep was in the line of flight and it hit the ground about five yards from the jeep. The shell must have finished off the man who was begging for help because he had been standing just across from the jeep and he went down.

I was sure the shell fragments had punctured the jeep tires, and I walked back to the jeep and looked at the tires and was amazed that they were still inflated. I called to the medic and told him the tires weren't hit, and he replied "Good!" Then I turned and walked back to the tank, walked around it, and stood on the side opposite the direction of fire. I wondered what was taking so long to get this other fellow ready to go, when all of a sudden a shell came in to my left and caused a tree burst about ten yards away. I thought a giant hornet had hit me in the fleshy part of my left hip. I yelled at the medic that I'd been hit twice and the third time was the charm. "Are you about ready?" He told me to "Come on!"

As I started to move from around the back of the tank, my foot caught on a root or branch hidden in the snow and I fell face down. As I lay there, I thought they would have to go without me. I was reluctant to call the medic to come help me up because he and the rest of the wounded had been exposed enough. I thought I'd just have to lay there and be killed by degrees until some fragment gave me the "fatal lick." I felt if I had any chance, I would have to get up by myself. I wallowed around in the snow like a crippled horse and managed to get one leg doubled up under me, then I wallowed the other way and got the other leg under. By then, I was on my knees with my face still down in the snow. I used my good hand and arm to start pushing my upper body up. When I was in a crawling position, I was ready to try for it. If my back and neck muscles wouldn't catch me, it would be useless.

I gave a tremendous shove with my left arm and hand that propelled me up to about a 45-degree angle. As my upper body came up, I gritted my teeth and tried to continue. As my upper body weight was caught by my neck and back muscles, a searing pain shot through my neck and shoulder. For a split second I thought I couldn't make it, but I came erect anyway and that relieved the strain on my wound. When you're standing around doing nothing other than collecting scraps of iron to pass the time, you just have to get on with it.

I walked back to the jeep and everyone was ready to go. The medic was starting the motor. I gingerly eased myself into the seat because when you've had your gluteus mangled, even if it is to one the side, you treat this sitting bit gently.

We traveled up along the woods road for about a quarter of a mile until we came to another road. We turned left and went down the road toward the crossroad where our hole had been before we moved up.

By the time we got on this road, we were finally out from under the artillery. It was just like driving out from under a thunderous rainshower.

It seemed almost quiet and peaceful out here, but we could still hear the shells banging away just a short distance back in the woods.

We drove on until we came to the crossroad, then turned right to go down the road that went out across the field. As we turned right, I glanced at our old hole and thought this would be the last time I'd ever see it. It's funny even a damned cold miserable hole can become home after a fashion.

As the medic wrestled the jeep around a turn on the slick icy road, he was just beginning to pick up speed when I frantically yelled, "Slow down, slow down!"

He answered, "Whatsa matter, whatsa matter?" Those mathematical-minded bastards were not satisfied killing us all up in the woods, they were trying to finish off the wounded. I had seen the krauts putting time fire or air burst over this evacuation road. It was of no military significance to them, they were just doing it for the hell of it. Fire or air bursts were exploding while still in the air as we were trying to execute this road. If the bursts are proper distances from the ground when they explode, scrap iron rains down from above.

There appeared to be about 15 to 20 shells in each firing, and they were exploding simultaneously. The Germans had them zeroed right over the road, and they were now exploding about 20 or 25 feet high.

The medic asked what we were going to do, and I suggested we go slow and get up just as close as we can, then when a batch comes in we could make a run past their zero point before they could fire again. The medic agreed to this and I told him to watch the road and be ready. I would watch for the flak.

He drove slowly forward and we were getting closer and closer to where I judged the zero point to be, though in the dark and with the world covered uniformly white, this was quite hard to do. We were now beginning to get too close for comfort. The medic had slowed the jeep until it was just about bucking. I could tell he was getting uneasy, and he wasn't alone. I was just about to tell him to stop and wait a bit, but before I could speak that stuff blossomed over the road just ahead of us and it looked fearsomely close. I yelled, "Now!"

The medic slammed the jeep into second, and I know he put a dent in the floor board with the gas pedal. At first the jeep just shuddered and nothing happened, but all at once it got hold and leaped forward like a wild stallion gone mad. We promptly hit the ditch. He kept the gas on the floor and the engine was turning on all rpms. I would have let up on the gas to get control, but then he hadn't questioned my suggestion for getting us by this place, so who was I to try to back-seat drive for him?

We plowed down the ditch a piece, and the old jeep was really bawling. When he tried to ease it back up on the road, it literally jumped up onto it. We sailed across and were nearly in a reverse skid. The back wheels hit the ditch on the other side of the road, which caused the front end to slam around, and we were straight again. He still had the gas pedal down, and we were gaining speed all the time. Mangled bodies were flopping all over the back seat, but no one uttered a sound. For me, I had a death grip on the seat with my good hand and was hanging on for dear life. When we came out of the ditch on the left, we went down the road in a long dizzy skid and wound up in the ditch back on the right. This time the medic slammed it in high. Somehow he got that thing aimed down that icy avenue and we blasted.

Now I know a jeep is not too fast, but on a narrow country road that is nothing but a ribbon of ice, and wide open, at night, without lights, it's pathetic.

I thought we were about to reach lift-off speed and I just couldn't stand it any more, so I yelled above the roar of this half-guided missile and said, "I believe we made it."

He just fell off the gas pedal. I don't think he wanted to get killed in a wreck either. Besides, when you've taken the trouble to get yourself all shot up in a war, to get killed in a jeep wreck before you get to a doctor just ain't dignified.

As he slowed down, I awkwardly turned and glanced toward the rear. Just as I looked back, shells blossomed out right over the road about 50 yards back. The old kraut was mean and cunning, but we had trumped that little trick. We were home free.

As we rode on toward the aid station, I began to think of what lay ahead. Somehow I had gotten the idea that a wounded man in an Army hospital was in for a rough time — maybe from too many Civil War stories or old Western movies. I could never have been more wrong. I was about to step through another door into an entirely different world, a door that has always brought back warm memories. I was about to leave a world that was cold and mean, where men had to be brutal to survive, where man's will and loyalty was made of iron, and the object was to kill. I was about to enter a warm, kind world where a smile was ever ready and the touch gentle, where wills were also made of iron, but the object was to save.

Chapter Ten

The Aid Station, Evacuation, and the Hospital

WHEN WE STOPPED IN FRONT of the aid station, I eased myself out of the jeep. A medic came and helped me into the building and onto a stretcher, helping me to lie down, which was very painful. He then followed a procedure that I soon noticed was practiced on all the wounded, except for the critical cases. He cut away my clothes — it was impossible to remove them — dressed my wounds, and gave me a shot of morphine. Then he brought me a glass of water; I didn't know that I was thirsty, but I drank without question and found myself gulping greedily. It was the best drink of water I'd ever had. When I finished drinking, again without asking, he pulled out a cigarette and put it in my mouth and then lit it. He then went on to repeat this same procedure with the next man.

I would like to tell you something about morphine. For the

painfully and seriously wounded soldier, it is a friend indeed. Used in its proper way, it is a life-saver in alleviating unbearable pain. As is everything in nature, it has a good side and bad side, but it is an almost irrefutable law of nature that the better servant anything is, the more terrible a master it can become. The thing that makes morphine so valuable to the beat-up wounded soldier is the almost instant relief from pain; it helps to prevent shock, and it gives the wounded instant optimism. It is virtually impossible to be pessimistic while under the influence of morphine. Within the hour, I had been cheating death by a hair, not once but multiple times — cold, beat-up, wracked with pain and shock — and now that my pain was melting away I felt safe and optimism was flooding through me. A man who has gone through that experience just has to appreciate the finer points of life a little better than the novice.

Morphine is conducive to recollection, and as I lay there I began to think of all that had happened in the last few weeks. I still didn't know the whole story of the Battle of the Bulge, but had a rough idea of the general picture. We at Bastogne were in a position that made our part easier to evaluate, but the soldiers I felt for were those from outfits that had been slashed to pieces without warning, lost, split up, no front, no way of knowing where the front was if there was one. I imagine that many of these lost and disorganized units or individuals were unsung heroes of the first magnitude. Some of their acts will never be known because the people who could tell them are dead.

I knew that the Battle of the Bulge was a cold miserable hell, and I think that any man who went in there as a kid came out as a man. One thing that I do know is that many a mother's son went in there under his own power, and he was hauled out on a truck like frozen cord wood.

The Battle of the Bulge has captured the imagination of many writers, both civilian and military. It has been studied, "cussed and discussed," for indeed, it was a battle of many elements. There was modern war without airpower, there was modern war with airpower, there was mechanized war, and then there was pure infantry war — and combinations of each. There was guerilla war, there was massive war, there was war with great leadership, and there was war where men fought alone, without leaders. The Battle of the Bulge had everything except warmth. If there had only been one heat wave it, would have had everything.

Most soldiers who fought in the Bulge realized that during the fighting there certainly wasn't any glamor and that the men who fought were typical of the American soldier throughout our history. That old mule-headed cussedness possessed by our soldiers has always stood us well. The American GI has always been independent in nature, not given to spit and polish, but in combat give him a reason to fight and he will say, "They damned sure will not pass!"

I thought of my own personal part in the battle at Bastogne and felt guilty for not being a big hero, but then I was too scared to be a hero! If they had given medals for being scared I would have gotten one. Heroes never know they are going to be heroes until the occasion arises, and then they don't even know until someone tells them. I was only a "coal car" for a bazooka tube, and I had to content myself with the fact that every-where the bazooka went I was always with it. I was amazed, though, the way a man functions and reacts even though he might be so scared he can hardly stand. And in spite of everything — including unbearable pres-sures, a sense of humor and a sudden flare of the temper just seem to pop out.

I have thought of this night in the aid station many times over the years and what it had been like and reflected on several coincidences that had occurred that made everything fall into place. I thought of all the cold, the pain, the shock, and the fear that Cap might bleed to death. I thought of that naked feeling I had sitting in the jeep that made me move away just in time. I remembered the poor guy who had hoarsely whispered, "Some-body please help me, I'm bleeding to death!" and how he had been stand-ing right in the line of the shell that I carefully avoided. As I pondered this, I thought that war doesn't care. When a man in war is wounded, no mat-ter how bad, no one blows a whistle and takes him to the sidelines. No matter how much he suffers or how close he comes to dying, the scrap iron keeps coming. He may be hit again and may be killed after he has been wounded, and even after he dies, his body may continue to be hit. War doesn't care.

This had been a pretty busy night and I suddenly realized I was so tired. Gradually as the morphine made a soft cover for my bed, I wondered why they didn't bring Cap in.

Just before daybreak, ambulances were brought up on the outside and the medics began to carry out the wounded. There were so many casualties that I knew stretcher space in the ambulance would be at a premium. Since I had walked into the place, I called the medic who had dressed my wound and told him that if he would help me to my feet, I could ride on the seat next to the driver and someone else could have my place on a stretcher. He replied, "You just stay where you are, Mac, we'll make it." How well he knew. I was to lie virtually helpless for over a month before I could even turn myself over in bed. A slug the size of a thumb was resting solidly against my spine just below my neck, and I found out that such wounds can be rather troublesome.

They carried me out and loaded me into a waiting ambulance. I was then carried a short distance and taken into a big tent that was a regimental aid station. There sure were a lot of wounded soldiers in there. I was given a tetanus shot and some breakfast. Later that morning I was loaded again into an ambulance and we rode for many miles over the icy roads. Sometime in the afternoon, we arrived at an evacuation hospital and I was taken for X-rays and scheduled for surgery early that evening.

When they were ready to take me to surgery, I was given another shot of morphine, and by the time I got to the operating room I didn't give a damn if it rained or snowed.

Military hospitals are not so secretive and squeamish about what the patient sees or how much they tell him as in civilian hospitals. This is particularly true of hospitals dealing with the combat wounded. My X-ray was right there in the operating room and no attempt was made to conceal it from me. I saw the two slugs in me and knew why the damned thing hurt so bad.

The anesthetist, a medical Captain, set about cording my arm to try to get a needle in for the Pentothal. I never did have big bulging veins, and with what I'd been through I now had none at all. In spite of everything, he couldn't raise a thing, but by feeling and guessing he started at the elbow and went down. After several attempts he still hadn't hit one. He was a nice pleasant fellow, so he began to apologize for not being able to hit the vein. I was full of morphine, so I didn't care and I would say, "Aw, that's all right, Captain, I ought to have bigger veins."

He kept sticking and we both kept apologizing until we had tried everything including the wrist. My hand was hanging down and I noticed the vein in the back of my hand was standing out some, so I said, "Captain, why not try that vein?"

Well, the cold had chapped and deadened the skin in my hands, and with all the dirt and blood they looked more like a rhino hide than hands. The Captain very carefully placed the needle and gave a little push; nothing happened. He applied a strong steady pushing pressure; still nothing happened. He then backed the needle away from my hand and took a running go at it; the needle bent. When he had gotten a new needle, he started back up my arm trying here and there along the way. When he got back to my elbow, he finally got one.

I became dimly aware that I was back in the ward. The lights were off and it appeared to be late. I was so woozy that this was all very vague. For some reason I put my good hand on the back of my head and felt a big pool of sticky liquid that was up to my ears. When one is coming out of Pentothal, he is liable to say anything and I was no exception. I bellowed out, "Who put this damned sticky stuff under my head?" I lay there in an uncomprehending daze for a few seconds, when all at once there were a half dozen people around my cot. They had a flashlight, and the ward boys quickly lifted me to a half sitting position. I saw a big white compress flash over my shoulder, felt the pressure as it was applied to my wound, and realized that the slimy stuff was my own blood! A big bleeder had broken loose, and I had been bleeding to death while I slept. While they held me up in this awkward position and reapplied my compress I went back to sleep.

When I awakened, the light was streaming through the windows. It seemed warm and friendly. I was relatively free of pain, and I was as hungry as a sow bear in the springtime. I looked around and everyone was eating breakfast. Most of them were about through. A ward boy suddenly appeared and set a big platter of hot cakes on my stomach, with butter, syrup, and good coffee. As I dug in, man oh man, did it feel good to be alive that morning.

Sometime that morning I was placed in an ambulance and driven quite a distance again. Later that afternoon I was placed in a tent littered with casualties. I remember that for supper that night we had potato beef hash, piping hot, and well prepared.

One thing that I learned and liked about the Army hospital, was not being babied. One thing that a man cannot endure, is to be spoon-fed, no matter how incapacitated. Although I was flat on my back, could not use a pillow, or even be minutely raised, a guy would come up with a tray of food, leave it on my stomach, and casually say, "Here's some chow." He then went on about his business. Although I am a strong right-hander, it was much easier to flounder around left-handed and eat at my own speed and desire than it was to have someone sit there and try to spoon-feed me.

That night the wounded were put on a hospital train and we were taken back to a general hospital in Verdun, France. It was number 193-some-thing, and that hospital was to be my home for over two months. A hospital train is equipped with shelf-like brackets along the walls, and the stretchers are laid on those brackets just like boards. The nurse in charge of my car was a good and kindly soul, so it was with misgivings that I saw her start toward me with a quart jar with what looked like a 6-penny nail sticking out of it. I was about to be introduced to penicillin.

I had heard of penicillin, but I didn't know it was in use. It was green and yellowish and looked sort of like a thick clear soup. The bad thing about it was that it was so new and crude that we had to have a shot every two hours for three days. They sure used big needles, and I have seen braver men than me almost cry when a nurse would start toward them with that hollow "fencing saber."

When we got to the hospital in the middle of the night, they carried me in and put me in a room. I hadn't shaved in two weeks and hadn't had a haircut in three months; my hair was matted with blood and mud. I know that I must have looked like a "*boar hant*." One seems to get more conscious of the way he looks the closer he gets back to civilization.

I was so bunged up and sore I couldn't even turn my head, let alone turn my body. When they began to slide me off the stretcher onto the bed, I had my eyes closed tight and was clenching my teeth to keep from screaming. Finally, they got me straight on the bed and after the pain eased a bit, I gradually opened my eyes. There, ringed around my bed were seven or eight of the prettiest young nurses you ever saw! I remember thinking, "Hell-fire-damn, I died sure as hell, and somebody has slipped me in to heaven by the side door."

I really became very self-conscious of the way I looked, but they were flirting with me and fixing my covers and fussing over me till I felt like some big celebrity. I wondered why I was rating all this attention.

About this time another man was unloaded, and the nurses moved on to give the other wounded soldier the same treatment. And, then the next, and the next, etc.

They had it figured out all right. When the nurses hovered and carried on about those half-wild, half-civilized crazy knuckleheads, they couldn't wait to get well.

There was an MP who continued to hang around my room, and it turned out that he was calf-eyed over a cute little brunette nurse. By leaning against my bed so that he faced the door, he could get a glimpse of her as she went each way up and down the hall. I don't think she was giving him any encouragement, but that didn't keep him from wishing.

I asked the him if there was any champagne to be had, and he said there was, so I asked him how much, and he said five dollars. He agreed to bring us a bottle, so I gave him the money and the next night we had a big bottle of champagne.

The boy in the room with me was from the 502nd regiment of the 101st Airborne. I was from the 506th, so it was just like being with "home-folks." But since neither of us could move, the MP acted as bartender and that suited him fine because that gave him an excuse to hang around and maybe catch a glimpse of that cute little nurse.

In our weakened condition, the champagne had a positive effect, so after we had consumed the bottle, we were feeling no pain. I thought about how ridiculous this was, so I said to the boy from the 502nd, "Ain't this a hell of a note — three nights ago we were up in that frozen hell with no end in sight, and now here we're warm as toast, high as a Georgia pine, and with an MP for a bartender."

He replied, "Life here is so hard I don't know if we can stand it or not . . . but we'll have to try."

With wounds such as ours, the doctors would let them "ripen" about a week before they sewed you up. This allowed shredded flesh to slough off so that there would only be live flesh after you were cleaned out before stitching up.

During the time I was in this hospital I got to know the personnel fair-ly well. Major Buckner (or a name similar to that) was the chief surgeon in charge. He was a top-flight surgeon, down-to-earth, and a common-sense kind of a fellow. If you put a leather apron on him and smeared him with a little soot, you would have sworn he was a blacksmith not a sur-geon.

Mrs. McManus was the head nurse. My personal nurse was Miss

Morely. There also was Miss Scott, who gave up candy for Lent; Miss Tucker, who was friendly and freckled; Miss Coulon; Miss Horn; an older one that I can't remember; the one who caused the MP to go calf-eyed; and the night nurse, who should have been named "Saint Something" because that's what she was.

Sergeant Miller was the ward master; there was a friendly boy, whose name I can't remember; Tony was from Orange, New Jersey; and Lee, who owned a Coca-Cola franchise in the Carolinas. He would describe the bouquet and aroma of a bedpan as only a professional could.

When the surgeons sewed us up, they did the boy from the 502nd and me at the same time and brought us back to the room together. Gradually, we began to wake up from the anaesthetic, and we were a mess, trying to talk but getting all lost in emotions. It was like two drunks on a crying jag doing that mutual admiration society bit. The next morning, after most of the morphine had worn off, I was in so much pain I thought I would go out of my mind. When I begged for something to ease my pain, they told me I would have to wait for Major Buckner to make rounds, which was to be soon. In the meantime, I thought I would scream.

The Major came around shortly and they had to take off my pajama top, turn me on my stomach, and pull my pajama bottoms down to my knees. This was hideously painful, so while the Major was examining me I told him I couldn't stand the pain and I would never make it.

He consoled me and added, "I know it hurts, and the reason it hurts is because I took a round ragged hole and pulled it into a straight line, and this required deeper stitches to hold it together. It will fill in with scar tissue, then we'll let the physiotherapist heat and massage it out, and that way you'll have a decent scar. If I hadn't done it this way there would be an ugly hole there." Then he said, "But don't you worry, you can have your shot any time you want it."

They put on a clean bandage, put my pajamas back in place, turned me over, and a nurse was standing there with the needle ready. That's when I realized the blessing of civilization that gave mankind a chance to develop a medicine like morphine that could show such mercy.

This examination routine was followed every morning and it was always a painful experience. One morning when the team that stripped me down had left, the Major and his team did not directly appear as was usual, so I was left lying naked for all the world to see. It's not so bad to be naked in mixed company if they are doing their job, but to be left that way for the public to observe is uncomfortable.

I could hear some of the French girls that worked there coming down the hall. As they got even with my door they would check their speed, then really move on, and I could hear them giggling.

I finally bellowed around and got Sergeant Miller in there, but he said if he let a sheet touch those open wounds the Major would have a fit.

Out of the corner of my eye I saw Miss Coulon go by, and I yelled for her to come in. While she clucked like a contented hen to her chicks, she was folding a towel, but the only thing wrong was that she folded this little towel until it was about an inch wide. She laid it up and down my back side and ran out of the room giggling.

Most wounds would have had the stitches removed in a week, but because mine were under such a strain to hold this hole together in a straight line, they were left in for nearly two weeks. When the stitches finally were taken out, I knew some of those threads were a half-mile long, and it was very painful. If anything, the wound hurt worse.

During all this time I got by on two shots of morphine per day, but on some days I think I got three. All in all, the boy from the 502nd and I were on morphine close to three weeks, and we were hooked good.

When we began to think we might be taken off the drug, we would turn our heads away from the door and listen for the night nurse to come in. When we heard the hall door slam about six at night, we would then go into our act. We would pretend we didn't know anyone was about, and begin groaning and carrying on in an agonized manner. The night nurse would hear us as she went by the door, she would stop, come in, and ask in a very compassionate tone, "What's the matter, boys?"

You never heard such pitiful tales of tortured pain as we spread it on. This got us a shot for two nights, but that nurse's mama didn't raise any dummy.

The third night we tried this she said, "Now you all have had about enough of that stuff and it's time you got off of it; you're going to get hooked if you don't." Hell-fire-damn, we had been hooked for two weeks. That stuff hooks fast, and because it's such wonderful medicine, it should never be abused.

We begged around until she finally said, "Well, all right, just this one time, but this is going to be the last."

Directly she came back with the shots and after 15 minutes I still didn't feel relief. I asked my roommate if he felt anything, and he said that he was laid back on pink cloud number nine.

I knew then that she had given me sterile water, so I began to yell and she came back into the room. When I told her that she had given me water, she denied it and said that I had so much morphine in my system that I couldn't feel it any more. I told her that I didn't change that much in one night, but she refused to back down.

If you asked me if I had withdrawals, I would say, "I'm not sure; I was too busy walking on the ceiling like a fly to worry about withdrawal!"

It was a miserable night, and if anyone who has not tried drugs knew what I know, they would run at the sight. After about three days, my withdrawals were over. I have never cared for drugs since, but it is reassuring to know that the medicine is available when you need it.

Within this hospital, the combat fatigue cases that weren't too bad were allowed the run of the hospital. This helped them stay in touch with other patients and nurses and was conducive to their recovery.

I never saw a combat soldier who was not compassionate and understanding toward genuine combat fatigue cases. No one has much use for a phony, but if a soldier knows he escaped combat by using deceit, he is going to have to live with himself realizing that he may have seriously damaged his ego and self-respect. When he sees someone suffering from genuine combat fatigue, no doubt he usually counts his blessing.

The soldier who slightly wounds himself or puts on an act to get out of combat will have to live with that for the rest of his life. If he would only go to the medics and tell them he couldn't go on, it would be much better than living a lie.

I noticed a good many of these cases around the hospital, some carried fishing poles wherever they went, although the snow was real deep and it was bitter cold! When I saw this I almost laughed out loud, not at them, because that was tragic, but because I knew why they were carrying those poles. Below the town of Moulton, Alabama, where I live, are two creeks that run together to form one of the stems of a larger creek called Big Nance. When I was growing up, my buddies and I fished up and down these creeks every spring. The high spring floods would wash away the trash and leaves and the short, clean, green grass on the banks was a delight on those balmy, gorgeous days when we would catch and cook our dinner.

When the night cold would become unbearable up there in Belgium on the front, just what do you think I would think about? Why, I nearly wore out the damn creek bank, and I know I went up and down those creeks in my mind more than I ever did in fact.

Soon after we were taken off morphine, the boy from the 502nd was discharged. His wounds, though serious, were not as complicated as mine.

My next roommate was a soldier from the Japanese-American combat battalion. He had been admitted to have his appendix out, which the doctors proceeded to do immediately after they brought him in. The operation was soon over and he was back in the room. He had been given a spinal and now he was wide awake. When he had only been in bed for about 30 minutes, he sat up on the side and said, "I wonder if they have any ice cream around here?" Man, I thought, he doesn't want to be eating ice cream or anything right now! He sat there for about two minutes and said he would go look for some.

In about five minutes, he came back with a huge bowl of ice cream and sat there on the bed and ate it all! I noticed that after that "go-to-hell" medicine wore off, he didn't get up any more. It was amusing to see him on the third day, when the Major came in and told him to get up. You never saw such a pitiful look of disbelief at that request, but the Major made him move, and he quickly recovered.

There were several French girls who worked in this hospital, and two alternated cleaning my room each day. One was very nice looking and her clothes were always clean. She was friendly and good natured, and seemed to be the kind that would always do her part and be easy to get along with. Her shoes looked as though they had walked through a cow barn, but these people had been occupied by the German army for four years, and I realized they had to make do however they could. This girl loved attention, and I teased her endlessly when she was in my room.

The other girl that cleaned was a little older, and she wore wooden shoes. You could hear them all over the hospital and they were probably the only shoes she had.

After about six weeks I was shaky on my feet, but I finally got up enough nerve to try to walk down the hall to the latrine. When I went in, one of the French girls was mopping the floor. I expected her to leave the room and wait until I came out, but she just kept mopping. This baffled me, so I said to myself, "I've always heard that these damned French people are crazy so I'm going to find out." I walked toward a trough and she sounded like you had turned loose a room full of parrots. She ran across the room and grabbed me by the arm, led me to a stall with a door, while all the time shaking her finger at me and making a real noise. I just grinned and thought, "Well, now I know."

One day, while she was cleaning my room, she put her hands over the end of the mop handle, rested her chin on her hands, and with a faraway look in her eyes stared out the window. I asked her, "What are you looking at?" and she dreamily answered "My oz band." I looked out the window and there was this strapping fellow in clean neat clothes, with a beret on his head and the ever-present cigarette lounging in the corner of his mouth. I said, "Is that your husband?" and she, very lost in space, said "Yaz."

My next roommate had been a tail gunner on a B-26 Martin Marauder and he was from Iowa. He had about 40 holes in him, and had been blinded in one eye. They took his eye out on about the second day. That night, although he had morphine administered, the pain caused him to scream and thrash. I was afraid he would fall off the bed, so I would take a firm grip on his arm, telling him, "It's OK now," trying to reassure him. He would relax. An hour might pass before it would start all over again. I didn't get any sleep that night. His wounds had been caused by 20mm cannon shells, and he had about 12 or 15 just in his chest and abdomen. One morning when his bandages were being removed, the holes in his chest and abdomen suddenly spurted fountains of blood. I knew he would bleed to death in minutes, and I knew what to do to help, but I thought the Major would tell me to get out of their way. I need not have worried; at almost the split second the bleeding began, he threw me a big towel and said, "Give us a hand, Simms." He and I jerked the bed from the wall and within two or three seconds from the start, Sergeant Miller, Mrs. McManus, the Major, and I had our towels on his chest and were walking our fingers so as to get a finger over each hole.

When we got them all plugged, we just stood there, waiting for the blood to coagulate. It seemed as if every muscle I had would give out, but finally the Major said, "I believe that ought to do it." We very carefully lifted our towels, and sure enough, the bleeding had stopped. I never saw this happen again. This tail gunner was a nice fellow, and he was married to a very pretty girl. As bad as he was shot up, I never heard him complain; he took everything in stride.

I had been going to physiotherapy to try to loosen up my shoulder and re-educate some muscles so that I could lift my arm. Although still sore and shaky, I was getting better. I was surprised that I was given notification to ship out and go back on duty. I was in no shape to pull full duty, and didn't know what I was going to do.

On the 17th of March 1945, I was discharged from the hospital. While waiting for my time to get loaded in a truck for the replacement depot, everyone in the hospital came around to say good-bye. I had become very close to these remarkable people and it was sad to leave them.

Chapter Eleven

The Replacement Depot

*A*T THE VERY TIME a group of us were riding in a truck to a replacement depot north of Metz, my division was back at our home base at Mourmelon-le-Grand, receiving the Distinguished Unit Citation. General Eisenhower was there, as well as a representative of the President of the United States and other Army brass. This was the first time that an entire division had received this award.

I thought I would be at the Replacement Depot for only two or three days and then be sent on to the outfit. No one ever told us anything, but it seemed that they took their time about sending wounded men back to duty. Fresh replacements from the States would be sent on to the front the next day. People who have been hospitalized need this extra time to build up their strength because combat is physically and mentally brutal. At the Replacement Depot, I soon got to know other men who seemed to have things in common with me, and we began to socialize with each other. It doesn't take long for like-minded people to find each other.

I became acquainted with a young school teacher from one of the northern states, and since I had been trained and had worked as an athletic coach and teacher, we had some good discussions. One day while we were exchanging a little healthy griping, he suddenly became violently angry and exclaimed, "We wouldn't have this war if it hadn't been for that God-damned Roosevelt and Hitler. I think they were in cahoots and they started this war so they both could make a pile of money."

A red flag jumped up in my face and I thought, "I've got a full-blown Commie on my hands." But I answered him very casually saying, "Just don't leave out that damned Stalin, for he's in it with them; and in fact, he planned the whole thing!"

When he got over his shock over my response, he made some lame excuse to go off somewhere and he never let me near him again. Needless to say, this ended our discussions.

The Russians and the Americans were allies, but soldiers in Europe knew that this was only a fair-weather friendship. In spite of what the politicians thought, we knew that when the war was over, Russia's true colors would become clear.

At about this time we mostly loafed around and with very limited duty, we gradually got a bit stronger. Sometimes we would go on a short march, and other times go out in the field and have a "refresher course."

One afternoon, we were told that we had to fall in for retreat and be prepared to stand rifle inspection! This somewhat teed me off, as we had gotten spoiled from limited activity.

I don't know how rifle inspection is done now, but in World War II during rifle inspection, the soldier had to stand at attention with his rifle standing beside his leg. When the inspecting officer stepped in front of the soldier, the soldier would bring his rifle up to Port Arms and open the bolt and breech. The officer would look the soldier up and down and then in a slapping or grabbing motion seize the rifle by the forearm. When the officer began this motion it would cause his shoulder to twitch. At that moment the soldier would turn the rifle loose and drop his arms to his side. If the timing was just right, the officer would in effect lift the rifle right out of the air. If the soldier did not turn loose quick enough, the officer would feel a tug and that was bad.

In basic training, we had been told that this was the only time we could drop a rifle and let it hit the ground. In fact, it was encouraged because it helped make the inspection sharp.

I had wanted to drop a rifle on the inspecting officer since I had been first told about this, and I had come close a time or two.

When the inspection began, I saw that the officer was from the Infantry, so he knew the score. As he came down the line, by ear and out of the corner of my eye, I caught his rhythm and I knew if I didn't flub, I could beat this timing.

As he stepped in front of me, my nerves were strung out, so when he twitched, my rifle was gone and I knew it. The Captain grabbed a handful of air as I stooped quickly and caught my rifle just before it hit the ground. I straightened up and just handed him the rifle. He turned red as a beet and looked the rifle up and down and wasn't really seeing a thing. This gave me a chance to look him over, and I saw that he appeared to be a good fellow, so I was sorry that I had embarrassed him. Finally, his color came back and he smartly handed me my rifle while looking me in the eye. "Soldier, if every man could turn a rifle loose like that it would be a pleasure to inspect." I very smartly said, "Thank you, Sir."

The Captain then stepped in front of the guy to my left and I knew what was coming. He hit that guy's rifle so fast he nearly jerked his arms out by the roots. I almost laughed out loud. So, today, I can tell my grandchildren that I once dropped a rifle on an inspecting officer and that Captain can tell his, "I once had a soldier drop a rifle on me — but only once, now, mind you."

Some of us were horsing around one day telling riddles and showing tricks. When I was in school and we were studying physical conditioning, I accidentally stumbled on a way to make my heart beat ten or fifteen beats a minute faster, and then slow it back down. I could do this while talking and appearing to be relaxed. I proceeded to show off the technique. Several of the guys timed and tested me to see if I really could do this. There was a big fellow in this group who belonged to a tank battalion, and he seemed to be very well adjusted. A few times, though, he had let it be known that he hated the Army and wished he was out. I don't know if he was worried about going back into combat, or just didn't like the Army period.

The next day was sunny, but cold, so this soldier and I were loafing on the south side of an out-of-the-way building, trying to absorb some sunshine and trying not to get caught on some detail. We were just talking and killing time, when suddenly he said, "About that heartbeat business you were showing us yesterday, what about showing me how to do that?"

I said I didn't even know how to describe it.

"Well, he said, just try and see if I can catch it."

I told him, "You might try to use this to get out of something," and he came back, "No, Sir, I would never do that, it's just that you've got my curiosity aroused."

I then tried to explain it to him, and damned if he didn't catch onto the trick the first time. In a few minutes, he could do it as well as I.

Finally we went on to supper, and I thought no more about it. The next morning I missed him at breakfast as we usually ate together, so when I got back to the barracks, I asked someone if he had seen this particular soldier. He said that the fellow had just come back for his things and was on his way to the hospital. The boy had gone on early sick call while we were at breakfast.

The soldier added, "I think there was something wrong with his heart."

I though to myself, "That low-down SOB."

Chapter Twelve

The Forty-and-Eights

WE WERE PUT ON forty-and-eight freight cars (40 feet long by 8 feet wide), and we rode off and on for almost two weeks, as we were moved from place to place. First we went up across the Rhine at Mainz, then back through France, Luxembourg, Belgium, and back to Germany. While traveling about, we had plenty of C-rations, and a stove for heating them and making coffee. On nice days, we would spend the time riding along with our feet hanging out the door. On cold rainy days, we would close the doors and heat up the stove, and it almost felt cozy inside the railcar. Going through France, we stopped for a while at a small station that served several adjoining villages. You could tell by looking at the villages and the people that they were not prosperous — and besides, they had been occupied by the Germans for four years.

When our train stopped, it was only a matter of minutes until crowds of women and children had gathered and were begging without shame. It did not feel good to witness this poverty, and there seemed to be nothing to give them. I knew that what little I had in my pocket wouldn't be much. Suddenly, as if on cue, the air was filled with ration candy, chocolate bars, chewing gum, and cigarettes. It was like a hailstorm. This stuff had been collecting in our pockets for just such an occasion as this. Some of the guys would try to say that they only threw out this stuff because they liked to see the people scramble, but they were liars. You don't think they were going to admit to being softies.

Once when we were stopped in Belgium, there was a long steep street going downhill from the railroad crossing, and on this street a sizable crowd gathered, hoping to get something from us. We got caught up in the moment, and began to give away our C-rations. At one point, there was a short, white-headed old man, complete with frock-tail coat, derby hat, cane, and spats. As he stood there trying to catch a can of C-rations, one hit the pavement right by him and it was lined up perfectly to roll down that long hill. Well, the old man and a kid about nine or ten years old went down that hill neck and neck after that fast rolling can. It looked as if they would chase it all the way across Belgium, but the kid kicked in the "after burner" and scooped up that can just like a good shortstop would. The old man came stomping back up the street for all the world like a bantam rooster that has had his feathers ruffled.

In late April 1945, in Verviers, Belgium, I had started across the street one day when off somewhere behind me I heard what sounded like a soldier cussing like you never heard before. I looked around quickly because I thought someone had had an accident. But it was only a Belgian kid hanging real relaxed over a plank fence. Being an old mule skinner myself, it almost brought tears to my eyes; I had a pair of mules at home that would have understood everything he said. Joseph was 12 years old, and he brought little shaving mirrors to our billet to try to sell them and help his mother make a living. He was a handsome kid, always clean and neatly dressed, although there were small expert patches on his clothes. His father was a prisoner of war in Germany, and I knew that he was missing him.

Some "crackerbrain" said to Joseph one day that he bet he hung around the Germans just like he did the Americans. He immediately became angry and emphatically said, "I will have you understand that I had nothing to do with the *Boche*!"

Joseph spoke English like a scholarly professor, so I asked him how long he had been speaking English. "About six months," he told me. I asked him where and how he learned to speak English so well, and he said that he just picked it up from the GIs. I finally realized that he could also speak French, German, and English fluently, as well as some Polish and a little Russian. One day, I feinted at him in a roughhouse way, and he quickly responded. I roughed him around as I would my own nephews, and he was bubbling with laughter. It was plain that these occupied people had been deprived of more than food and clothing. After we would rough-house, we would sit on the side of my cot and talk.

From these talks I became aware that Joseph was one of the most intel-ligent people I had ever met, and that even included the grown-ups! I have wished many times that I had gotten his full name and address, so that we could have kept in touch.

One day without being prompted or questioned, he began to tell me about the affairs of the world. He matter-of-factly told me that the war would soon be over, that at the time the United States was the strong-est nation on earth. But, he warned, just as soon as the war would be over, the U.S. would get rid of its military might just as quick as it would be possible to throw it away. Joseph said that when the U.S. speaks now, the whole world listens, but after the U.S. has thrown away its military might, when she speaks no one will listen. The U.S. is the leader of the world whether she wants to be or not, he added. It will be bad for world politics if the U.S. does not stay strong and exercise this leader-ship.

Joseph continued, telling us that Eastern Europe would go communist by force, because it would be occupied by the Russians. There would be a great campaign to try to get Western Europe to go communist, by political means, with Italy and France being the most likely targets. And when the U.S. gets rid of its military machine, then the Communists will start little trouble spots that would cost them little, but cost the U.S. much. They wouldn't go far enough to risk Russia itself getting into war, he predicted, but the little wars and incidents would have a draining and demoralizing effect on the U.S. And once this war is over, Joseph told us, and the U.S. becomes weak, the trouble spots would start and they would just go on and on.

Needless to say, I have had reason to think of Joseph nearly every day since World War II.

When political experts speak of power vacuums, what they really mean is that the pecking order is not in place and things will not reach a stable condition until it is. This is true in all mammals, and maybe more so in man, for if any group of men form an organization, be it small or consist of entire countries, it won't be long until everyone finds a comfortable place in the pecking order. In animals and man, if the top dog or leader abdicates his position for whatever means, everyone becomes dissatisfied until the order is reestablished. Little Joseph understood this so well that it was really elementary.

One day, our train was stopped at a street crossing in Belgium and a bus pulled up to a stoplight so that its front door was even with our open box-car door. As the bus was waiting for the light to change, one of the most beautiful girls I have ever seen turned in her seat and looked straight toward us. A boy who was standing casually by the door of our train looked up, gave a startled yelp, jumped about ten feet out toward the bus, hopped on the bus, sat down by the girl, and was spreading his line before the light had changed. If ever I saw a man look up and recognize at first sight the girl that he intended to marry, this was it.

Chapter Thirteen

The War Is Over

THEY PUT US BACK ON THE TRAIN at Verviers, Belgium, and sent us up to Münster, Germany. After we had been there for a few days, a false report was spreading like wildfire that the war was over.

I was billeted on the third floor of a large building. The room on top had very large windows, and when the GIs in town began to fire their weapons, this room offered a good target for a stray bullet. There were enough weapons being fired to equal a hot fire fight on the front, and therefore some of us on that third floor stayed away from the windows. We had survived the war and we didn't want to get killed by a stray bullet. The war ended for me here in Münster, and the ending seemed anti-climactic.

When a country has been caught up in war for so long, it begins to seem like a way of life. It was such a strange feeling, and I'm sure the feeling was mutual for other soldiers. I would catch myself thinking, "You mean I went through all that, I'm still alive, and it's all over?" A soldier can't help himself from reflecting on the battles he has fought, after he has survived a war. Most of us have tremendous self-doubt. I had plenty before, during, and after I was in combat. If I had known in advance how bad combat was going to be, I don't think that I would have survived it. But now that it was over, I was almost surprised at myself, because I had probably engaged in the biggest battle of my life and I had won. This biggest battle was not with the Germans, but with myself.

When I look back, I now see that I stood up and behaved in a manner that was better than I ever thought possible. I did this in spite of terrible fears, the brutality of combat, and the tortuous cold. I now can say that I went through "trial by fire" and passed the test.

It's been said that to be mentally healthy, one must like oneself. When you go through combat and come out mentally and physically intact, then you have to respect yourself.

I have reflected on the fact that I was glad that I lived in a country that respected, and had feelings for, the individual. The cold almost got my feet, but if they had gotten any worse, I could have told the medics and they would have taken me back.

This is in contrast to what I saw back at the hospital. Several trainloads of German soldiers had been unloaded at the hospital on stretchers. These men were being brought to the hospital for one purpose, and that was to amputate their feet, which looked like overripe and cracked-open black grapes.

These German soldiers had been forced to stay on the front until they were captured — not to try to win for a just cause of some kind — to satisfy the ego of a total and heartless fool who had no mercy on anyone but himself. If Hitler had only committed his last act — suicide —ten years earlier, what a blessing to the world it would have been.

We were soon put on trucks and sailed down the Autobahn through the industrial part of Germany, past Frankfurt, and on down to Worms. This Autobahn, or superhighway, was ahead of its time, but it had been built for the express purpose of the fast deployment of armies.

When we got to Worms, I thought about Martin Luther and the

Protestant Reformation and how long ago it had been. It, too, was for the express purpose of trying to bring about a little more freedom of choice and a little more "say so" of the individual.

While at Worms, I met a soldier that I had known in basic training. Back then he had been young and shy and not quite grown-up. He now seemed older than his years, but he had a hearty, well-met kind of personality. I would have never recognized him, but we had a great visit after he spotted me.

From Worms we went down the highway toward Berchtesgaden, where our division was headquartered. We went through Stuttgart, Ulm, Augsburg, and Munich. The sights were the same everywhere; almost all the big cities had been reduced to rubble. Proceeding down the Autobahn, we crossed the Danube and the Inn Rivers.

We went over the ridge of the Alps that takes you back down into the valley of Berchtesgaden, and I *almost* wished I was back in combat. This highway just hung on the side of the mountain and you could look down for a thousand feet, and up for a thousand feet — but you'd better not go sideways! Riding in the back of an open truck under such conditions with some half-baked knucklehead driver nonchalantly pouring all the coal he can get to go through the engine was almost worse than combat. "Oops, look out! Boy, that scared my mule. Whew, I thought we were gone that time."

We got to Berchtesgaden at night and we bedded down in the lobby of our division headquarters. The solid floor felt good after that ride around the mountainside. The next morning they picked us up and we went into the Salzach River valley. We followed this river until we came to a small town called Lend, Austria. This was where my company was stationed. The whole division, in its occupation role, was scattered all over hell and half of Georgia!

The Salzach River was small, but beautiful, and although it flowed fairly swiftly, it was shallow and was always totally covered with ripples.

There were snowcapped mountains in every direction and between the valley floor and the snow line, the slopes were covered with evergreen forest, except where it had been cleared for pastures. The valley was quite narrow here at Lend, but in places it widened out into farm crops, such as hay.

Lend consisted of a group of buildings on both sides of the river with a picturesque bridge across the river at this point. I guarded jet plane components and other things in Lend, but generally I was posted on roadblocks, and one roadblock in particular.

There weren't thousands of displaced persons in Europe, there were millions, and it seemed as if half of them came through our roadblock. They were coming mostly from eastern Europe to go to Italy, to Innsbruck, or to cut back north and go up into Germany and beyond. Some were German soldiers in uniform, coming in to give up and be processed and discharged, others had been the enemy's slave labor. The common denominator of this mass of humanity was that all they wanted to go home.

Sometimes the brass would have us turn them back temporarily, which would greatly upset them. They had gone through so much suffering that any delay in their quest for home was almost unbearable.

Many walked, others had confiscated horses and wagons and rode in them; the lucky ones rode in old cars. All of these people had to have their identification checked, as did the immediate local population.

When German soldiers came along, we would keep them with us until we went off duty, then take them back to town and keep them in a room next to the our bunk. We didn't post guards on them, as we wanted to get the processing over as quickly as possible.

The roadblock that I manned was about a quarter of a mile down river from Lend. The highway was on the right of the river and a railroad track was on the left. At the site of this roadblock, there was a swift stream running through a gash in the road and into the river. Back up this stream about 200 yards was a waterfall that kept up a subdued roar. There was a ten-foot drop down a steep bank to the river's edge, and a wooden bridge spanned the stream that ran through this deep gash in the road. It was a beautiful place, and this was where I spent most of my days and nights, two hours on and four off.

We worked these roadblocks in pairs, and it was totally informal. We sat on makeshift stools, and the officers never bothered us, which was good. We checked the bulletin board for our scheduled time to be on duty, and it was just like going to work. There was no guard muster, and if there was an officer or Sergeant-of-the-guard, we never saw them. We were required to carry a loaded weapon at all times, because we still couldn't be sure that some die-hard German SS outfit wouldn't cause some trouble.

When the truck that took me there dropped me off at the Command Post, someone in authority pointed to a building across the river and told me to go there and find a place to pitch my gear. I crossed the bridge spanning the river and going around the corner of the building, I met Dick Taylor, Menholtz, duPont, Wieder, and McCollum from my division. We all started laughing and shaking hands, and they said they didn't think they would ever see me again. I immediately asked them about Cappaletti.

"Cappaletti is dead."

I asked what had happened, as the medics had him the last time I saw him. It turned out that the medics got hit too, and in the chaos of the night and the savage artillery barrage, it was daylight before caring for the wounded could really get back on track. But by then it was too late for some.

In our off-duty time, Taylor, Menholtz, Wieder, McCollum, Jacques duPont, and I liked to roam around up in the mountains. We did a little "fishing" with German grenades, until Wieder wound up like Bob Feller and missed the creek.

We had a Sergeant DuPont, who was to become our First Sergeant, but PFC Jacques duPont was the one that amused me the most. No noncom that ever called roll could pronounce his first name. They would call him Jake, Jack, and Jock, and a few other things. When they would start calling out names for a detail, I would cut my eyes at Duke to watch him cringe, but if you wanted to see him come up out of his shoes just let some whangy-voiced Corporal sing out "Jackie duPont!"

We were all PFCs. Some said the PFC stood for Poor _____ Civilian, and anyway, if it was work detail we caught it. The outfit had captured a bunch of "happy hour juice," but it was almost all gone when I got back. Some of the men had found barrels of liquid up in a warehouse that smelled like cognac, and if your imagination was strong enough you might even think it tasted like cognac.

Just before we left the valley in July, someone finally got the medics to get this barrel checked out, and it turned out to be fluid for tanning leather — but it never killed anyone, and we blissfully didn't know this for about six or eight weeks.

One morning several of us walked across the bridge to a local barber shop to get our hair cut. I think it was Vernon Agy who had some of the brown juice in a bottle, and he gave it to the Austrian barber, asking him if it was cognac. The barber took a big swig and said, "Prima cognac, prima." I guess he was doing one last good deed for der Führer.

Chapter Fourteen

Occupation

*T*HE FIRST DAY ON THE ROADBLOCK, there was some slack time in the flow of people, during which a girl on a bicycle rode up and stopped. You talk about a knockout, this was one. She could have graced any magazine cover. She had pretty dark hair and a peaches-and-cream complexion that make-up would have *damaged*. She had a figure to match, and a relaxed and friendly personality. And she always wore a bright red dress.

Many of the local people could speak some English, so I thought I would have a little conversation with the living doll while I was checking her pass. But she could hardly speak any English, and for some dumb reason I said, "*Parlez vous Francais?*" At this, a torrent of French came pouring out of her, like water out of a pitcher. Of course, I had to admit that I couldn't speak French. But by using a few words of French, German, and English, she conveyed that she had been born in France and that French was her first language. Soon she went on her way, and I had no idea that a scenario had been triggered into action.

When locals came through, and we knew them by sight and that their passes were OK, we would wave them on, as it saved time and effort. They didn't dare try to go through unless they were waved on, because some of our soldiers were mean as hell and would just like an excuse to shoot someone. When the girl in the red dress came back down the road from Lend, I told my partner, "I know who that is coming in the red dress." Before she got to us, I waved her through, and this "turned on the footlights" and "raised the curtain." Just past us down the river, a concrete wall kept the mountainside from washing into the road, and on down this road was a blind curve.

The girl in the red dress would come from around this curve, riding along casually, but, when she got to where she could see us clearly, and if she saw that I was on duty, she would go into a zany act. She would lean down over the handle bars like a French racer from the *Tour de France* and begin to peddle furiously. By the time she got near us, she would be sailing. If I was sitting down I would raise a leg, and wave her on and if I was standing, I would use my rifle barrel but in plenty of time so that she wouldn't be uncertain of my intentions. Just before she reached the wooden bridge, she would put her feet and the pedals in the coasting posture. As she coasted to the bridge, just as the front wheel touched the first plank, she would yell at the top of her voice, "*Parlez vous Francais?*" I would quickly bellow, "Chevrolet coupé," at which time with this bit of crisp lunacy out of the way, she would put the pedal to the metal and away down the highway she would fly.

She played this little game with me every day that I was on that roadblock, and sometimes several times a day. To this day I can't think of that amusing scene without smiling.

To get to my room, I had to go through the large room next to mine with the German soldiers. One day, as I was passing through, an older German followed my movements and caused me to think that he wanted to say something. Finally I decided to stop, and I spoke to him. He could speak fairly good English, and we began to have a long conversation, trying to understand each other's differences.

He told me, "Hitler has destroyed our country."

I knew the answer to the question I was about to ask, but I wanted to hear his version. When I was in the eighth grade, Hitler had come to power, and our Current Events class had been doing a thorough job of studying him and Germany, to the extent that the boys in my class knew that Hitler was going to provide us with a free ticket abroad, and he did.

I asked, "Why did you all ever let him get such a hold on Germany so that he could do what he did?"

"That is the easiest answer of all," he said. "You Americans think you had a depression, but yours was minor compared to ours." Then he told about Germany's inflation where wheelbarrows full of marks were necessary to buy a loaf of bread!

In my small home town, many people out of work in the cities came home to the land owned by their parents or grandparents and rode out the Depression by trying to stick together. We survived on taters, turnips, free rent, and patched britches.

The German soldier said that Hitler had promised to put bread and butter on the table, and he did just that. The German population had more jobs and food, the economy was looking better, and Hitler was a great leader that was going to save Germany. Furthermore, with all the hustle and bustle, the building of the superhighways, and factories, times seemed to be good. He went on to say that "We didn't know the crazy son-of-a-bitch was building these roads to run his armies on, and by the time we found out what he was really up to, he had the Gestapo in place and we were afraid to open our mouths, even to our own families."

Many people thought that Hitler had charisma, but that is not necessarily so. Charisma is a possession of qualities of leadership that causes people to have unswerving attraction and allegiance. Those who have this gift are usually natural-born leaders. People with delusions of grandeur do not as a rule have charisma, they are too busy taking themselves too seriously. Hitler had power, due to his brutality, deceit, and terror, but in the end he destroyed his people, his country, and himself. Before he came to power, no one would give him the time of day. He had few friends, and he was a loner and a loser. But he had delusions of grandeur and an insane desire to rule all of Europe, not only for what the world had done to

Victims of Nazi brutality. The scene doesn't seem to change from Hitler's Death Camps in 1944 to Bosnia and Kosovo in 1999. *From The Epic of the 101st Airborne: A Pictorial Record of a Great Fighting Team (101st Airborne Division, 1945)*

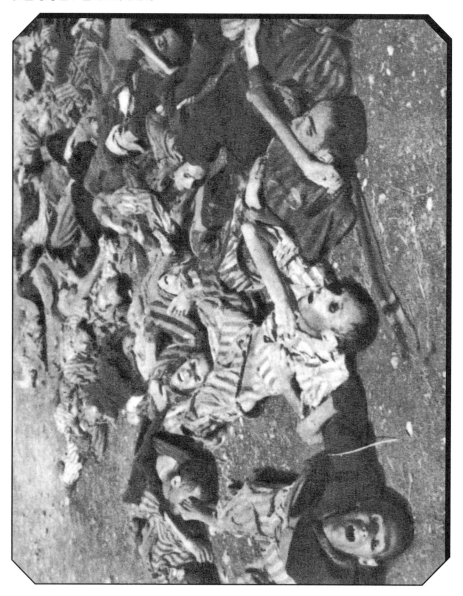

Germany after World War I, but to get even with the world because it didn't recognize him for his great talents. He intended for all to know who Adolf Hitler was.

Hitler gained his power by organizing bands of thugs. Some of them might be educated thugs, but thugs they were at heart, and it was not the burning ambition of Hitler that attracted them, but the rewards of power and material gratification.

Hitler is known to have said, "Strike fear into the people, and show no mercy." His growing numbers of thugs, went about the business of spreading the fear, and they got away with it because the existing German government in power was so weak. When Hitler got the backing of the "Junkers," who were the ruling or upper class from which the officer corps had always come, then he was ready to press for power.

The officer corps had been put down after World War I but Hitler told them there would be another military, and you will rise to the top like cream on milk and take your rightful place of position and power. The German soldier confirmed just about every negative thing that I had ever heard about Hitler. When the Führer whipped up people with street speeches, it was not charisma, it was demagoguery. What many people do not realize is that everywhere that Hitler went, his Brownshirts also went, watching the people in Hitler's presence, because the unpardonable insult to Hitler was any kind of disinterest. If the people were in Nuremburg Stadium, the way to keep the watchdogs from suspecting them was to holler with all their might, and that would cause the watchers to look elsewhere. The people had to *pretend* to be enthusiastic about Hitler. This all had an isolating effect on anyone who was against Hitler, because they had no idea who their like-believers were.

Make no mistake, if Hitler had charisma, it was like that of a cold frog. He was one of the cruelest degenerates ever to disgrace humanity.

One night while McCollum and I were posted on a roadblock, an Army truck stopped and dropped off a well-dressed, distinguished-looking man and his very pretty daughter. Our trucks did this often, as our guards could help these people catch another ride, give them directions, or take them somewhere when the trucks and guards went off duty.

Mac and I had our usual small fire going, and as we greeted the man and young woman, the man told us he had slipped away from Prague, Czechoslovakia, and was hitch-hiking to Paris with his daughter. He had a plan to present, with representatives of other Eastern European countries who had agreed to try to ease the burden of being occupied by the Russians. The man carried a thick manuscript that had all the technicalities and details of this plan. And he was using the expression "the Eastern Bloc Nations" frequently. It was too hard to see much of the report by campfire, and the details looked *brain-breaking* anyway. The gist of the plan, as I got it, was something like this: The Eastern Bloc countries would have an agreement to cooperate in some ways to try to put up a solid front that would be stronger than one country alone. The man was taking this to the Allied Command in Paris in order for them to put pressure on the Russians to agree to some concessions, or at least to accept some restrictions during their occupation of these Eastern Bloc countries.

I don't know how much success the man had with the Allied High Command, but I did hear mention in the news after that of the Eastern Bloc countries.

We finally wore out this discussion with our visitors and just sat around the campfire warming our hands in silence. Directly he said, "This is just like out West." I didn't have the heart to disillusion this good and earnest man so I just said, "Yep, it sure is."

And that perhaps is why he was so open about showing me all this highly confidential material. In the Hollywood Westerns, the "good guys" always win, but also the "good guys" could always be trusted. It was a good feeling that these far-off parts of the world had an image of Americans as the "good guys."

During this time of occupation, there was a 12-year-old boy who lived in the building next to the one where I stayed. He was a husky friendly boy, who seemed very intelligent and was willing to do a good deed. One day Dick Taylor happened to mention that he would like to have an Edelweiss flower, and he was somewhat pleasantly surprised the next day when this boy handed one to him. The boy had climbed the mountain and got one for Dick.

This German boy could speak English, though not very well, and I had several conversations with him and I thought that we got along great. One day he and I were just sitting around talking about things in general, and we began to discuss the way that Germany had been torn and destroyed. Just as an explanation, I said that Hitler was bad and it was his fault. Well, I might as well have stuck that boy with a red hot pin because he reacted quickly and positively. He told me in no uncertain terms that it was the fault of Hitler's no-good assistants that Germany had come to this humiliating defeat, that Hitler was good, and that Hitler was his Papa.

This took me by surprise, because I knew it couldn't be so, but in trying to translate this and remembering that Hitler said he acted with divine guidance, it seems as if the boy really meant that Hitler was his spiritual father. He went on to say that Hitler was perfect and could do no wrong, and therefore Hitler could not be the cause of Germany's destruction. It was impossible to reason in any way with this boy where Hitler was concerned, and I knew that I had run into one of the "children of Hitler," Hitler Youths who had had their minds stolen. Put anything into a child's mind when he is young enough, and whether it's true or not, he'll have a hard time ever getting it out.

The older soldier that I had talked to earlier was grown when Hitler came to power. While he could pick Hitler to pieces and see where all the false logic had been, this boy had his reasoning power tampered with at the time of his most important development.

Since that conversation with the boy, I have never ceased to deplore the fact that a person would steal the mind of a child, imprint it with false doctrine, and mess him up for the rest of his life.

There is no doubt that many of these children of Hitler would never be able to discuss him in a logical or objective manner.

The difference in soldiers reared in a free world from those reared in places where they steal the mind of the young is something like this.

If in World War II a Russian officer had told a soldier, "Charge across that field and die for Stalin," the soldier would have charged across the field and died mainly because he would rather be shot from the front as from the rear.

If a Japanese officer had said to a soldier, "Charge across that field and die for the Emperor," the soldier would have charged across the field and gone on to join the Rising Sun.

If a German officer had said to a soldier, "Charge across the field and die for der Führer," the soldier would have charged across the field and gone on to that glory hole they were so obsessed with.

If an American non-com had told an American soldier, "Charge across that field and die for the President!" the American would have said "Kiss my foot!"

American soldiers do not die for Presidents. The American soldier dies for what is his, his home and family, his sweetheart, his ole hound dog, his fishing hole, pool hall, ball team, theater, and all the other things that are part of the little piece of the world that make his life worth living. The things that the American soldier fights for are very real and when this world that he holds dear is threatened, then you have a very motivated soldier — and that's the reason that even generals used to say that the American soldier was the sorriest garrison soldier and the best field soldier.

When you say "your country" to a young American soldier at war, his mind will automatically dart to an image of his home; and when he sees the flag, that's kind of like dog tags that identify this place where he can live his life and do his thing.

I have a friend who said that he had noticed that he and all his friends and relatives never mentioned patriotism in their World War II conversations and letters; it was always about girls or what they were going to do when the war was over. I said, "What the hell do you think they were fighting for?"

While we were in Austria, we didn't get enough to eat to satisfy our constant hunger, and some of us had a craving for a meal of fresh fish. One afternoon, McCollum and I got up a fishing line or two, and set out down the road. We were not supposed to talk to, or fraternize with any of the German villagers when we were off duty, however no one paid much attention to this regulation. It was a silly rule anyway, and subsequently had to be discontinued.

Walking down the road, Mac and I stopped by a house where a man and his wife were working out in the yard. We tried to ask them about a good place to fish, but they didn't understand any English at all, so we were getting nowhere. At this time, two Lieutenants came along riding horses, and when they saw us talking to these villagers, one of them proceeded to chew us up one side and down the other. He ordered us back to town, and as we started on the way, they rode on in the opposite direction.

When they had gone around a hill, Mac asked me, "What was that all about? I could see where he might get after us a little, but he didn't have to be that rough." I told Mac that I had sassed that Lieutenant up on the front and, apparently, he was just getting even. Many shepherd dogs that get kicked by a cow will go back and bite the guilty cow, even if she has disappeared in the herd. After that he will leave her alone.

I will admit that I sassed him, and I will testify that he bit back, and after that, he was as friendly as could be.

When the officers got out of sight, Mac and I climbed over a fence and hid till they came back and passed our hiding place. We then got back on the road, and went fishing!

Early one morning, about three o'clock, Dick Taylor and I were working the roadblock by the little bridge. We had been saying that it was worth it to be on guard duty just be present in this beautiful setting. There was a big bright moon, and it was bouncing right off the snow-covered peaks like a pinball machine gone crazy. The river appeared like thousands of little dancing mirrors; the waterfall was playing its base fiddle; and the evergreen forest acted as a stabilizer. The temperature was extremely pleasant, and it was just a good time to be alive. I just didn't see how anything could be any better than this place or this moment in time.

Gradually, however, we became aware of a strange sound coming from around the blind curve down river. As the sound got nearer, it proved to be a goodly number of small musical tinkling bells. When this sound became louder, we realized it was a small herd of cattle, each with it's own little tinkling bell. Behind the cows was a horse-drawn wagon in which sat a man and woman with a young baby. When the man stopped the wagon, the cows all stopped, and they and the horses stood perfectly still, except for some slight head movements. When the cows moved their heads, the little bells would lightly tinkle, and each cow seemed to take a turn, and then there would be a duet occurring.

The man got down out of the wagon to have his pass checked, and with the moonlight so bright, we could almost do this without our flashlight. Meanwhile, all this natural beauty was displaying itself and the cattle were putting in their little tinkle's worth. The woman very softly, in the clearest most beautiful soprano, was singing "Lili Marlene" to her baby as she gently swayed it to and fro. While Dick was checking the man's pass, I was entranced and wished this could go on forever. But presently, the man climbed back in the wagon and they went on their way.

The cattle and horses made practically no sound on this smooth road, so we could hear the singing and the bells as they left. It gradually faded away until there was silence once more.

I turned to Dick. "Taylor, what we have just witnessed could never be captured on film as we experienced it." Dick had been thinking that same thing.

On another bright morning, when my partner and I were working the roadblock by the waterfall stream, word was passed down for us to turn back all civilian traffic. I hated these days because these displaced people wanted to go home so badly, and to be stopped was a terrible blow to them. We turned back a few, and it was not pleasant to see the look on their faces when they had to go back the way they had come.

Soon an old man walked up, and I believe he was about as weary looking as I had seen. He was carrying his belongings in a small pack, and he pulled out his pass without being told to do so. He appeared to be in his fifties, and he had a little stubble of gray beard.

When I told him he couldn't go through, but would have to turn back, his chin began to tremble. I have never seen such a dejected look of bitter disappointment. All at once I said to myself, "To hell with the brass; they don't have to look these people in the eye, and besides this old man's pass is in order, he's not hurting anyone, and it makes little difference whether he's on the road this side of Lend or the other."

I barked "*Achtung!*" and he instantly braced himself at attention and his body began to tremble. It just scared the living hell out of him.

When he was at attention, I traced my eyes back down the road from the direction he had come. Then I looked up into the forest above and beyond Lend. I moved my eyes back down to the road, and then raised them into the distance.

When I completed this, I asked him in German if he understood. He began to whimper in a fearful manner, and it was plain that he was completely bewildered. And he expected me to knock hell out of him because he couldn't understand.

I again barked "*Achtung!*" and he braced himself again. I repeated the eye and head movements, and then I grinned at him and asked him again in German if he understood. This time he didn't tremble and whimper; he just looked at me with blank wonderment on his face, as if he was saying to himself, "Did I just hear and see what I thought I did?" His face began to brighten and little by little it turned into a beam. All at once he burst out laughing, and he grabbed my free left hand with both of his and he tightly hugged my hand to his breast, all the while saying, "Thank you!" over and over in German.

I never saw such carrying on from a grown man. I never heard so many *Danke*'s and *Ja*'s and laughing and gurgling. I thought I was going to have to cut my hand off and give it to him for a security blanket, since he was about to hug it off anyway.

If anyone wanted to get technical, they might ask why I didn't follow instructions, and the answer is that the decisions we made on those road blocks were judgment calls at the best. Someone might want to know why I let this man pass, because for all I knew he might have been a war criminal trying to slip through. This is the easiest answer of all.

War criminals did not have calluses on their hands; they put calluses on other people's hands. I noticed when he pulled out his pass that his hands had about the thickest, hardest calluses that I had ever seen. Someone had been doing a very good job in seeing that this old man didn't while away his time in idleness.

I just stood there like a grinning ape and let him scratch his happy place for a while, but soon in mock anger I told him to get the hell on back down the road. But, he wasn't scared of me now, and he would just hug my hand tighter and laugh and say thank you some more. Finally I got him to leave, and the contrast was really something. When he first came up to the roadblock, he was so tired he had to force one foot in front of the other.

When he went back down the road, he was walking like a 16-year-old, with springs in his heels.

For the rest of my tour of duty that morning I knew the old man was in the forest behind us trudging happily along as he by-passed our road block on his way home.

Chapter Fifteen

Bruck, Austria

URING THE MIDDLE OF June 1945 we had been moved upriver to Bruck, Austria. The valley widened out here, and about a mile beyond was Zellam See, which means "beautiful sea." Anyway, Zellam See was on the shore of a big lake, Zeller See.

Bruck consisted of two clusters of buildings, and the road that crossed the river at the first cluster went up a small gentle hill for about 100 yards, then down a gentle hill for another 100 yards to the other cluster. The road, or a branch of it, went on to Zellam See.

I was billeted right by the bridge, where the road from Lend came into Bruck and crossed the river. One day we were having a formation up at the Command Post, which was a small building at the top of the gentle hill between the two sections of Bruck. As I came out of the building and started up the road to the Command Post, it soon became apparent that most of the company was already gathered up there and every man was looking straight at me. I glanced around to try and see what they were looking at, but I saw nothing.

Quickly, a jeep emerged from the group and began to move slowly down the road toward me. I knew that the jeep was the key, but I couldn't connect it all until suddenly I saw two stars on the bumper. It was General Maxwell Taylor.

The General's jeep was about 40 yards away, as I began to look up at the group with a half smile, craning my head a bit as if I were looking to see if someone in particular was up there. I was trying to act as if I didn't know that the jeep even existed. I guess by this stage in the war I was reaching a bit of the "devil-may-care" attitude toward some of the brass. When we were about 30 yards apart, I could see General Taylor's face. He was boring a hole through me. All his clones in the jeep were also looking mean. When the king laughs, his court laughs; and when the king frowns, his court frowns.

The driver had the jeep just barely moving, and I continued to look up the hill. Just before I became even with the front bumper, General Taylor looked like he was going to eat me for lunch. But I quickly popped a snappy salute to him, as if it was just such a routine thing for me to salute Generals, that it was almost an afterthought.

I know General Taylor saluted a lot of people, but I wonder if he ever popped one to anyone as snappy as the one he popped to me.

When I got up to the Command Post, Agy was laughing as I walked in. "It's a good thing you saluted that jeep because if you hadn't, General Taylor would have chewed so much of your backside that there wouldn't have been enough left to make formation."

I asked what in hell was going on up there, anyway.

Agy laughed and said, "Everyone was standing around laughing and talking, when General Taylor's jeep drove up in their midst. No one paid any attention, or called attention, and the General just sat there. Finally, when the General was sure that no one was going to pay him any mind, he started cleaning off a new ground, so to speak." Agy said that when the General had "eaten all the meat" he could hold, he looked up and saw "dessert" — me — coming out of the building down by the bridge.

Though Agy and I weren't "bosom pals," we saw each other when we were just loafing around the billet. When I had joined the 101st Airborne Division in France, one of the first things I noticed was that we had a "character" in the outfit by name of Vernon Agy, and anytime there is a character in the neighborhood there will be some odd things happening.

The small town and community where I grew up had more characters per square foot than any place I've ever seen. Journalists might say that characters make good copy, and that's true, because those who are a little different from the average person add the salt and pepper and other spices to the general routine of life.

I had been around these "characters" as I had grown up, and because of the interest they could create, I had always enjoyed them and was glad that they enriched my life. Some of them made you cuss, some made you laugh, some even made you cry, but all of them made for good conversation.

Agy, one of these "characters," had told me about his own little experience with General Taylor. In Holland, the men had not received an air drop with provisions, and they were about to starve; they were living on apples and anything else they could find. So, Agy left his rifle at the Command Post and went off to the local area, scrounging for food. He found a bakery where there was an abundance of those long slim loaves of bread, so he stacked all he could across both arms until he was having to balance them with his chin. When he went back out in the street, the first person he met was General Maxwell Taylor.

General Taylor asked, "Soldier, where is your rifle?" Agy replied, "It's back at the CP, Sir."

General Taylor looked straight at him and then slowly shook his head from side to side as if he couldn't believe this was happening.

Finally, the General said, "Soldier, if you stay in this man's Army for another 150 years, don't ever let me catch you without your piece again."

I asked Agy, "What did you say?"

"I said 'Yes, Sir,' very meekly."

We hadn't been in Bruck very long when Lieutenant Hatfield took a truckload of us up into a high valley to the south, in order to occupy a small town for about a week.

We took a cook with us, and although he only had dehydrated food to work with, he made our chow taste better than what we got in the mess hall. We had little meat though, and everyone was hungry for it.

As far as being on duty was concerned, nothing much happened in that town and nothing passed through. Instead of handling crowds of people, now we only sat around on our guard post and took up space.

One day I decided I would go farther up in the mountains and try to get a deer to supplement our meager diet. I looked out the window and surveyed the area off in the distance, and observed that up high near the snowline there was a very steep forested belt around the mountain. Directly above this belt the mountain shelved or benched over, and that made the forest going around it almost like level or gently rolling ground.

Animals seek out the easiest place to walk, so if a game trail was up there, it probably would be on that benched area. Later that afternoon I set out and, in trying to save walking, I took a short cut, which resulted in a very hard climb.

By then, I was hot and tired and was looking for a good place to sit and rest a bit. Suddenly I came face to face with a small boy and girl.

I could tell they weren't frightened of me a bit, and so I smiled and sat down on a boulder. They also sat down. The girl sat very properly to one side, but the little boy sat on the boulder and squeezed himself up tight against me.

She was a pretty child, about ten years old, with a faded dress that came to her ankles. He had his front teeth missing, so I suppose he was about six. They had been up in the pasture to get their cows.

When we were comfortably seated, I gave each of them a piece of chewing gum, and when the little boy got that gum going real good, he suddenly grabbed me in an affectionate bear hug. He turned his face up to me with his eyes squinted and gave me that hideous snaggle-toothed grin that only the young know how to make.

I had known this kid for only about five minutes, but that didn't make any difference to him. I patted him on the shoulder and thought to myself, "All soldiers probably look the same to you, but there's a lot about being a soldier that you don't know and if you're lucky you won't ever find out." I knew they had to get their cows, and I needed to continue up the mountain before it got any later in the day, so we waved good-bye and parted ways.

Soon, I came to a steep forested area that was so strenuous I had to use the trees as braces to help me climb. Then suddenly the steep incline benched over and it was like looking out through a forest on level ground — and before me was the game trail that I had expected! It appeared to be used very little by humans, and it was probably hundreds of years old. The thick needles from the evergreens kept the trail padded, and it was not worn down or eroded. I sat down on the trail and leaned against a tree to wait for a deer.

I didn't have long to wait. Soon a young buck appeared about 75 yards away, and was coming down the trail toward me. He only had two spikes and was colored somewhat like a white tail deer, and had a light gray face, with brown and gray on his back growing lighter underneath.

When he was within 15 yards of me he stopped, as he saw that his path was blocked. Since animals are attracted more by motion than bulk, I remained perfectly still, and he was not the least bit alarmed. I didn't try to shoot him at that time, but was curious to find out what he would do.

Since I was blocking the trail, he simply moved off of it a foot or two, and began to walk on toward me. As he passed behind a tree, I shifted my rifle slightly so that I would be in-line as he came abreast.

He still came forward, almost even with me, and then he stopped, stuck out his nose toward me, and with his great eyes glistening and nostrils twitching, he tried to stare me down! With my own big eyes abugging, I was meeting him stare for stare. I could have patted him on the nose with-out leaning, and all I had to do was slightly move a finger and we would have meat for supper.

The whole atmosphere overtook me — "younguns" in your lap and now the deer, what the hell — I let him go. Presently he sensed something that alarmed him, and he took off. At the angle he was running, I could still down him with ease, but I just thought about all this for a bit then got up and went on back down the mountain.

I got there just in time for chow. The cook had managed to whang up the best supper we had eaten since we had been there. I really did enjoy my meal that night, and without deer meat. I'd had worst days.

Not long after we were back in Bruck, I was in my room alone one afternoon, when First Sergeant DuPont came rushing in.

"Simms, get your rifle, you have to go on guard duty tonight. The crazy SOB who's supposed to be is falling down drunk, and I've got to have someone. You're the only one I could find."

I nearly hit the ceiling. This was my day off. But I got my rifle and went on down.

This post was on a long drive that went from the road up to a big castle that had been occupied by Hermann Goering. There was a riding stable and in the castle all kinds of art and antiques that Goering had stolen from across Europe. I believe that it had the best-stocked wine cellar in all of Europe. This was Goering's vacation retreat where he brought many of his like-minded friends. Goering didn't follow Hitler because he believed in the politics so much, rather he loved the spoils of the rich life it brought him.

Our battalion officers had pitched their sleeping bags in this castle and made it their home. Standing guard, we *almost* felt sorry for them because we knew that they must be very bored in there and probably didn't have anything to do at night but play cards.

I had been on the post only about five minutes when I saw a soldier coming down the road. Although it was July, he appeared to be wearing an overcoat, so I said to myself, "I bet that's the drunk I'm supposed to relieve of duty."

Sure enough, he came up and told me he was ready to relieve me. He seemed to be somewhat OK in his speech, but his legs and "auto-pilot" seemed to be non-functioning. I told him that Duke had put me on for the night and he could go on back to town. But he didn't want anyone to have to do his duty.

By this time, a jeep came up the drive and in it was Lieutenant Colonel Hester, our Battalion Commander, along with several other officers. The jeep stopped and Colonel Hester, looking straight at me, asked, "What's going on here, soldier?"

Now the drunk leaned forward a little too much and began running all the way across the road, and the officers braced themselves because it looked as though he was going to run headlong into the jeep. But he caught himself partway over, just at the last minute, and then he made the mistake of trying to go back across the roadway. He wound up going down the road backwards with his feet jumping up in the air and his back and head almost down.

He caught himself again, and when he straightened up, he tried to be real dignified-looking, but, of course, he repeated the whole procedure. He ran up and down the road at these odd angles while I was trying to talk to Colonel Hester.

When the Colonel had first asked me what was going on, I had tried to beat around the bush a little, but the Colonel would have none of it and he repeated, "I said, 'Soldier, what is going on here?'"

I thought, "To hell with it, I'll just play it straight because that's the best," so I said, "Sir, this man was supposed to be on this post tonight but shortly before changing of the guard, my First Sergeant came and told me I would have to take this post tonight. There has been a little misunderstanding, but I think we about have it under control."

The Colonel popped me a snappy salute, and said, "Very good, soldier, carry on." Then they left.

Jacques duPont was another of the "characters" I had met in the service, a friendly and likable cuss who also had a great sense of humor. One thing that he and I completely agreed upon was that neither of us was interested in having any rank above PFC. We were constantly wary that the awesome authority that goes with being a PFC would corrupt us and tempt us into abusing our power!

Late one afternoon, in Bruck, Austria, Jacques approached me on the street and asked, "Simms, do you know where there are any taters? I'm starving for some fried taters. I have a skillet, a stove and some lard, but I can't find a tater in this whole durn town."

"My good man," I told him, "you have come to potato headquarters!" There was a large patch just down the highway between our location and the castle, and I had been watching the crop closely, and they were about ready to grabble.

Jacques naively asked, "You mean you can get them before they get ripe?"

"You are looking at a man," I explained, "who would have died in his infancy from starvation, had it not been for grabbling potatoes in the springtime!"

As Duke sensed that he was going to get his fried taters, he began to drool and carry on, so I said, "Watch that Pavlovian stuff." He said, "I'm not thinking about Pavlov, I'm thinking about fried taters."

I hate to bring Pavlov up so much, but the principle he discovered is forever entwined in our habits whether we realize it or not.

I had Psychology under a "Pavlov nut" but when I found out what it meant, I realized that farm boys knew all about it. When you pull the left line of a mule and yell "Haw!" the mule soon gets the message.

I told my professor that if he thought Pavlov's dog cut up when he heard the bell, he ought to see a damned crazy mule in the middle of a cotton field when the dinner bell rang.

Old Duke was chuckling and grinning and stamping around in good form as was his habit when we were making "much ado about nothing."

I told Jacques that when darkness would spread its "cloak of secrecy upon this wretched land," we would go forth on our crusade against hunger! And so we did. At dark, we walked down the highway and when no vehicles were coming, we slipped out into the field. I showed Duke how to scratch a potato out, then refill the cavity so that the plant would continue growing.

We soon had enough and went back to his room and quickly had a big skillet doing its thing. When we were through, we were like pet pigs — a little greasy, but content. To this day, every spring, when I dig my garden potatoes, I get hungry for fried taters and I can see Duke's face.

One night, some of us were off duty, lounging around in Sergeant DuPont's room, when we fell to discussing the shortage of good "ruckus juice."

"Well," Duke said, "we still have that stuff in those barrels." To which I replied, "But Duke, that stuff is so rough that it's hardly worth it."

We had quit calling this stuff "cognac," as the barber up at Lend had called it, but we still didn't know it was used for leather tanning.

Duke said he had figured out a way to make it better, and like all good cooks who try to give you all the details of a dish so you will brag on them, Duke proceeded by saying, "I take a quart of that stuff and pour it in a pan, and I add one-half pint of water, then I squeeze in six lemons, and then I put it on the stove and bring it to a hard boil, at which time it will become almost as clear as water." Then he added, "When you do that, it's not too bad." But his voice sorta had a wistful tone, as if somewhere in his dim memory a bourbon was trying to surface.

I had heard that Sergeant DuPont and Captain Wilson, our Company Commander, had both gone to Gulf Coast Military Academy, so I asked Duke if he had gone there and he said he had.

I asked him if he knew a certain person and he said, "Yes, he and I were good friends and played ball together." I told him that I had roomed and played football with this boy in college. That made it kinda like old home week.

I then asked him if Captain Wilson had also gone to Gulf Coast Military Academy.

About this time Duke had poured himself a big glass of that doctored-up leather tanning fluid and was just about to put it to his lips, when I asked him about the Captain.

He went ahead and gulped about three big noisy swallows, at which time his lip went into a tight banded spasm. His eyes pulsated three times, but because his lips had such a tight grip on his mouth, his goozle only jumped up twice. At this time he stiffened as if he had turned to stone for a full 30 seconds.

Finally he dared to try a little bit of his lips over at the side of his mouth and he sort of Bogarted and said "He was my rat."

I said, "You mean Captain Wilson was a freshman and you were an upperclassman and Captain Wilson had to shine your shoes and run errands for you?"

Duke by then had gotten his breath, and with it came the joy of being able to speak again, and he said, "When I squalled, Captain Wilson jumped!"

I then asked him, "Do you and Captain Wilson ever talk over those old times?" and he said, "Hell, no, he don't mention it and I'm scared to."

Another night, I had again caught guard duty at the entrance gate to the courtyard up at Goering's "rented" castle. It was misting in the late afternoon when I went on duty, and it promised to get heavier.

There was a guard hut at the gate, so that the guard could stay dry when nothing was going on. Shortly after I took my post, a field grade officer and two Lieutenants came out to my post and told me that a Polish Count and his wife had been keeping house for them, but they had to banish the Count from the castle. They warned me that the Count would probably return and try to talk his way back in, but I wasn't to let him in under any circumstances.

I think it turned out that the Count had been trying to steal some of Goering's loot, but I didn't know any of the details. The officer made it clear that the Count would really like to work his way back into the castle, but he said, "If he gives you any trouble, just work him over with your rifle butt."

The three of them went back into the castle, and I was left alone. I thought to myself that if the Count was all that persistent, I might just have a piece of work on my hands. But the officers lived there, as did the officer of the guard, so if that's what they wanted, so be it. Personally, I dislike a lot of confrontation and, therefore I wasn't looking forward to seeing the Count.

Nearly an hour had passed, and the rain was getting heavier. I was hoping that the old Count wouldn't come by on my shift.

About the time I thought I might not have to deal with this, a "long drink of water" came sauntering up the driveway, as if he were out on a springtime stroll. The gentleman had on a white shirt with no tie, a pair of golf knickers, checkered socks that came to his knees, and a pair of black slippers on his feet. His dark hair was combed back, and he acted as if it wasn't even raining. He casually walked up and started through the gate, ignoring me all the while. I stepped in front of him at port arms. He spoke excellent English, and said that there were a few personal things that he wanted to pick up in the castle, and that he would come right back out.

I told him that I had orders not to let him in. The rain by then was coming down steadily, and I wanted this over so that I could get back under shelter.

The Count argued more aggressively, but I wouldn't give. All at once he attempted to step around me, but I quickly moved in front of him and positioned my rifle so that if he tried it again I could take his chin off.

I thought for a minute he was going to persist, but finally he said, "You're not going to let me in?" and I said, "No way."

He stood for a moment, then he turned and left. I was relieved that the confrontation was over, then was surprised to see he had walked over to a three-foot high wall that bordered the drive.

Laying down flat on his back on top of that wall, the Count pulled one knee up and crossed his legs, then proceeding to serenade me with Polish folk songs for a full half hour. He seemed to be totally oblivious to the rain pouring down in his face, and I actually pinched myself to make sure of what I was seeing. Finally, he got up and without so much as a backward glance, he strolled off into the dark.

Chapter Sixteen

Agy and the Captain

F ROM THE BEGINNING, one thing I'll say for Vernon Agy, I never heard him speak of Captain Wilson in a hostile or angry manner. Most of the time he was laughing. If Agy was tempted to do anything that might not be by the book, which was often, and if he could get away with a caper without worrying the lesser brass, he would do it! One day Captain Wilson called Agy on the carpet, and during their discussion Captain Wilson said, "Agy, I'd court-martial you if I could but I can't." Translated into plain English, it meant, "I know you're guilty but I can't prove it." Agy would relate this to us later, and would just break up with laughter thinking he got away with another masterpiece of tomfoolery. In the latest session they had, the Captain "put the wood" to Agy by making him pitch a pup tent right by the Command Post and sleep there every night.

One night a group of us had been at the other end of town hanging out, and as we were walking back up the road to our quarters, we passed the Command Post. Agy left our group and dropped off at his quarters, the pup tent. Someone asked about service at the Waldorf. He said, "Go to Hell."

Soon, however, we had to pack up our gear, and we were loaded onto passenger trains and returned to France. I was sure glad we went by train because I don't think my nerves could have withstood another wild truck ride around the side of those cliffs. We were subsequently stationed in a town not too far from Paris.

We had unloaded our gear and were assigned to our quarters, but there was no Agy to be found. Captain Wilson had gotten his revenge. Agy had been transferred to the 17th Airborne Division!

When we had been in France about two weeks, Captain Wilson had been on a pass to Paris and when he arrived back in town, one of the other officers went to pick him up and this is what an eyewitness said took place.

The officer meeting Captain Wilson said, "Captain, I'm afraid I have bad news for you," at which time Captain Wilson jumped up, shook his fist at the sky and yelled, "Don't tell me, I know, that damned Agy is back."

Agy not only had gotten himself transferred back, but to his company and platoon. When Agy heard what Captain Wilson was supposed to have said, he was "hot dogging" just like he'd made a touchdown.

While all this was happening in France, I heard from my cousin who was also stationed in Europe. He and I had grown up together, not only in play but in work. At 16, I was farming a two-horse crop on our little piece of acreage, and my cousin was doing the same on his family's, about a half-mile down the road. We had swapped work and helped each other a lot that year, and sometimes during the middle of the week we would put up a keg of home brew in a pine thicket near one of my fields. It would "come off" at the weekend and be ready to drink. Mama almost caught us once, and I guess there would have been hell to pay, but we lived to get grown-up.

I recalled the time we had together. Once we were racing our horses while standing erect in the saddles and going around a blind curve on a narrow country road when we met a wagon and almost joined the shadowy realm. We had been in and out of a few places up and down the "road of life."

I received a letter from him telling me about something that happened while he was in basic training. In a town near his camp one night, he met an especially cute girl and made a date with her for the next evening. What Cuz didn't know at that time was that she was from a one-parent family — just a father — and that in itself was enough to make her daddy as paranoid as a rattlesnake. In addition, because this girl was so cute, the soldiers had been hanging around like flies around a molasses spill. Add to this the fact that some of these soldiers had given her daddy a lot of static, and when he saw a uniform, he began to salivate like a dog who has just reached the active stage of rabies. By the time Cuz stepped into their living room that night, the daddy had already worked himself into a rage by just thinking about a soldier coming to call.

He began to cuss Cuz and tell him about a lot of disagreeable things in life, then he pulled out a big gun and rammed it in Cuz's stomach, telling him in no uncertain terms that he was going to modify Cuz's body structure.

Cuz said that the father kept raving, so he finally said to the man, "If you've got nerve enough to use that thing, use it, and if you haven't got enough nerve, just shut up." Cuz said, "I looked him right in the eye while he emptied that thing through his living room floor right in front of my feet."

Cuz went on to say, ". . . After that me and that old man got to be plumb good buddies. When I would go to see his daughter, he and I would drink a beer together, and we just had a good old time while I was stationed there."

When I read Cuz's letter, a wave of nostalgia swept over me. I wrote back at once, "Cuz, don't you write me any more letters like that, you know they make me homesick." And he didn't.

Chapter Seventeen

"War Stories"

*O*NE DAY SOME OF US were talking about the combat action on the night that I was wounded. The men were pretty sure the artillery began when a "Scared Rabbit" picked up a booby trap on his shovel. When the trap went off, the German artillery began almost immediately, and he assumed that the explosion had given the Germans our exact location. The booby trap had wounded some boys nearby, but "Rabbit" didn't get a scratch. "Scared Rabbit" was 25 yards away looking back and running at the speed of light when that thing blew.

Most soldiers try to put on a front to conceal how scared they are, but that day, old "Rabbit" didn't give a damn who knew he was scared or how badly.

One of our "corn shuckers" from Iowa told us that later on that day the battalion pulled back to our previous day's positions and he and "old twitch boot" were assigned the hole that Cap and I had been in at that crossroad.

On the uncovered end of the hole where we had been standing guard, the earth was packed as hard and smooth as pavement. One of the men — Dale — bragged what a good hole it was and how conveniently it had been fixed by a V-1 buzz bomb, called the "terrible Vergeltungswaffen — the weapons of revenge, the V-weapons." The buzz bomb was a small unmanned aircraft with a bomb in its nose. The buzz bomb was powered by a pulse jet that made a hellacious sputtering noise. It traveled on autopilot to its target, and when it reached its destination the engine would cut off and the plane would dive so that when it hit the ground it was just like a bomb. When one of these buzz bombs was in the clouds — or if it was night — you couldn't tell where its exact location was, and the sound it made would make the hair on your neck stand up.

Dale told us that he had just come off guard the night the buzz bomb hit, and old "Scared Rabbit" had just stood up in the end of the hole. About the time Dale was about to doze off, he heard the buzz bomb coming. At the same time, old "Rabbit" grabbed him by the leg, frantically asking "What'sat, what'sat?"

Dale told him it was just one of those old "buzz bombs." He warned him that when the motor cuts off that means it's about to fall. Just at that instant, when the rocket was about overhead, the motor stopped.

"You may think I'm lying," Dale told us, "but that damned boy's feet were going up and down on that hard-packed dirt so fast that they sounded like teeth chattering. I thought if I just reached up and grabbed his belt from behind, give it a tug, turn it loose and holler, boo, he would scratch a trench all the way to Paris."

When the bomb hit and bounced the ground up and down, "Scared Rabbit" was just about a basket case.

I am almost positive that every combat outfit has a "Scared Rabbit," and I think that in the long run they are good for morale, as I don't know anything else that provides so many laughs. Pop Davis recalled that when old "Rabbit" got a lick on his head in an accident, a nurse in the hospital where he was treated said that she believed that the lick on his head had affected his mind.

Pop said, "I could have told her, by Gawd, his mind was affected afore he got hit."

One day a boy came running into our barracks, laughing and trying to talk at the same time. He said, "I just saw something so funny, that you won't believe it."

Colonel Robert Sink, our Regimental Commander, he said, had come over to our area, gone into a shed where a soldier had set up a barber chair, and sat down to get his hair cut. Now, Colonel Bob Sink was not just like your usual run-of-the-mill "chicken Colonels" that you meet up and down the road. Just after the war was over, a good many soldiers slipped off and went AWOL to do a little celebrating. The disappearing soldiers were such an embarrassment that a division staff meeting was called to try to deal with the problem. When the figures were added up, one of the Regimental Commanders said, "Why, Bob, you have more men over the hill than anyone in the division." At this, Uncle Bob replied, "Them's my boys!"

At any rate, when the barber had put the shawl around Colonel Sink, it covered his uniform, and if you didn't know him by sight, he looked just like any other older soldier. But about this time, a young "pup" came in, and being new in the outfit, he didn't know the Colonel from Adam's house cat. As he sat down, Sink asked, "How's the world serving you, soldier?"

The boy very animatedly replied, "Them stupid bastards are running me crazy."

The Colonel responded, "Who are you talking about, son?" At this the boy opened up and said, "Them sonsabitchin' officers, they ain't got sense enough to come in out of the rain."

One of the witnesses to this encounter told us the boy elaborated on the ancestry of officers in general, and very plainly implied that they all engaged in some very repulsive activities. And while the boy was carrying on, the Colonel just grunted answers and never let on as to his rank or his identity.

As luck would have it, the boy was so agitated that he bounced up and went on his way, and as far as I know he never knew who he had been talking to.

The next morning, however our bulletin board had a memo posted: "From now on all Company Commanders will be responsible for seeing that their men know the field grade officers of the regiment by sight."

On August 7, 1945, Dick Taylor came running into the barracks.

"Simms, they've just dropped a bomb on Japan equal to 20,000 tons of TNT!"

He was talking so fast I was not sure I had heard right. He slowed down a little as he repeated himself adding, "It's got to be the atom bomb!"

I remembered a passage in my high school chemistry book in 1937 that had stated that though some people think the atom can be split, releasing a tremendous amount of energy, it was not in the foreseeable future.

The future turned out to be eight years later!

Although we had been scheduled to eventually go to the Pacific, we all believed that the war was as good as over, and if the Japanese didn't surrender at once, there would be more bombs.

The bomb brought us together and had us thinking in an entirely different manner. We knew that our lives were going to change, and that we would be on our way home.

This old gang of mine was about to be broken up — Pop Davis and Mitchell, the racehorse rider, from Texas; McCafferty, who wanted to fight the Russians; William Davis, a gambler from the Big Apple; Sergeant Meighs, from the mortar platoon; Basinger, the one who tried to wound a Tiger tank with a .30-caliber machine gun; Miller, the fine musician; Shield, from Idaho, who used to measure the snow pack; Dale, the "corn shucker" from Iowa; James Putman, a contractor from Amory, Mississippi; and Thomas, a young member of our group that I met later in a hospital in Florida. And there were some faces that today, many years later, remain without names and some that probably have been overlooked. But none of these guys have ever been forgotten.

Our feelings were bittersweet, like graduating and leaving high school, knowing we would never really be together again. I think everyone had come to the realization that this shared experience of war was coming to an end. We had gone through hell together and we were alive, unlike many of our friends, and we had developed a special kind of loyalty and understanding amongst ourselves that none of us would forget.

Chapter Eighteen

The Victors — and Readjustment

FROM THE TIME I was sent back to duty in March 1945, until I was discharged from the Army in 1946, I had been in hospitals, replacement depots, and with my own division. Everywhere I went, I talked to soldiers who had been all over Europe and they represented many outfits and a cross-section of all parts of the U.S. Most of these soldiers had several things on their minds and one of them was Russia. Russia was "bad news" to our boys. Some of the soldiers were very positive about going right back into combat, saying they would volunteer if the U.S. would declare war against Russia, while we had our military ready. This may have seemed crazy to some people, since we had fought so long and hard and had lost so many men, but these soldiers considered our victory hard won. And the threat of Russia profiting by acquiring territories won by our soldiers was not acceptable to the veteran.

Many of our boys thought that Uncle Sam and the folks back home had done a wonderful job of supporting the soldiers and providing the matériel necessary to win the war. And they hoped that the sacrifices that had been made to win this war would be that last great ultimate sacrifice and the last war ever. They hoped that the government would be up to the horse trading that lay ahead, and that future generations of Americans would honor the sacrifices made.

Dozens of times I heard many enlisted men who had seen combat state that the folks back home can never understand what we had been through.

It's true that a person who has never been in war can never fully understand what war is like. We all had the same self-conscious awareness about how to relate to the folks back home the hell that is war. It was a human slaughterhouse over there, but you just don't walk into a room full of civilized people and tell them that.

In many of our discussions, the men said that the people in the U.S. didn't know how well off they were. We had thought that growing up during the Depression was hard — little money and lots of work, but compared to the war in Europe we were living in a paradise. We just didn't know it. The soldiers I talked to all seemed to think that when we got back home, the folks there and the returning GIs should count their blessings and try to be good friends and neighbors, be satisfied with what we had.

And we always seemed to return to the subject of family and home towns, and the way we were brought up. "Mama's cooking" got a lot of mileage. Things that the men had done with their fathers, usually referred to as the "Old Man," got a good bit of attention. One guy said that the only reason he wasn't in the penitentiary was because he figured that if the penitentiary was any worse than the "Old Man's" razor strop, he didn't want any part of it.

But "Mama's" discipline was a little different. "Mama" had a lot of give and a lot of toughness, and the more stories you heard, the more they all seemed the same. Mama wasn't too hard on you if you played it easy. In fact, she would help keep the "Old Man" from finding out things sometimes. But if you pushed Mama too hard and got her stirred up, she would tear your behind up in a minute!

If the parents of these battle-scarred soldiers had heard themselves being bragged about, they would have glowed, though these men probably wouldn't have been caught dead letting their parents hear them. On the other hand, maybe the parents wouldn't have been caught dead bragging on these young hellions they had reared.

We had a good time talking and thinking about home and the good life ahead.

The one thing that caused more disgust than anything that I heard while overseas were the so-called "readjustment" lectures that we attended before we were discharged. I participated in at least three or four of these, and I never heard so much griping and outright hostility toward any speaker by those soldiers attending.

Someone behind a desk had come up with the brilliant deduction that the war had turned us into trained brutes. We were too dangerous to be turned loose on society, without "readjustment!" After attending two or three of these lectures, which I thought were simple-minded, we would be "recivilized" properly, and could be returned to American life.

Frankly, I never saw a soldier who had come through with his mind intact who couldn't put the battlefield and his civilian life in proper perspective without even trying. If they wanted to know how civilized we were, they should have observed the enemy children and how they trusted us instantly. The mothers did not worry in the least when their kids played with and hung around American soldiers. But one of these readjustment experts that I had read about earlier had come up with that theory about combat men getting sleepy when they're in a bad situation because they want to sleep to escape. He wasn't smart enough to realize that after going for about four days and nights without a wink of sleep, and thereafter only an occasional catnap, I had had a very damned good reason to be sleepy in combat and it wasn't to try to escape into some fairy tale.

After the war was over and everyone returned home, I would still ask other veterans questions that would help me answer some of the most perplexing aspects of battle. And one of the questions would be, "When you hit combat, how long was it before you could sleep?" The answers would usually be anywhere from a day or two up to a week. A friend of mine who was in the Marines in the Pacific said, "I don't know if I ever slept; I could hear a pissant crawling a half mile away and if he got careless and crawled over a dead leaf, I would call in artillery!"

Chapter Nineteen

Back to the Hospital

*A*LTHOUGH MY WOUND was still terribly painful when I left the hospital, it had become a little better while we were down in Austria. The two things that got the most exercise while we were there were our feet and mouths! But when we got back to France, it was a different story.

Usually, ordinary training just gave me an appetite, and was no big deal, but now it was something else. We began to train to keep in shape for possible future duty in the Pacific, and when the war with Japan was over, this training was continued, supposedly as a means of keeping us busy and preventing us from getting too mean and bored. But the result was that all the training aggravated my wound to the extent that normal sleep was impossible and I experienced severe pain 24 hours a day.

I went on sick call to see if there was something that could be done. The Medical Captain that examined me was a combat man, and he understood wounds, so when he got through I was surprised to hear him say, "I don't know if anything can be done, but I'm going to let the hospital decide."

At the hospital, a physical therapy team headed by a Major went over me with a fine-toothed comb. Later, the Major came up to my ward and told me that after a consultation, the other medical team was in complete agreement about me. Because of the nature of my wound, it would be impossible to exercise the soreness out; it would only make it get worse. They determined that I needed at least six months or more of almost complete rest and recuperation to become completely well, and then we would go from there.

I thought I would get a paper that would allow me to get light duty or some flunky job. But I was surprised to find myself before another board of doctors who ordered me sent home! But, somehow, I was assigned to the same general hospital I had been in after I was wounded the first time. It was in a different town, but had many of the same personnel. Something was odd, though, because everyone that I ran into always said, "What are you doing here?" I didn't know what to make of this until I met up with a boy that I knew fairly well. He told me that I was supposed to have gone back to the States when I had left the hospital, not back to training. It turns out someone in personnel had goofed up and got my name on the wrong list. If no one had checked back with the Major, he would not have known the difference.

I had wondered about this, because the Major had worked with me and had showed me how to walk my fingers up the wall and concentrate on different muscles in order to learn how to lift my arm. I was barely learning this when I was sent back to duty. And when I got back to the division, they had no record of me. It was as if I had never existed. I was the only person who knew where I was! My service record had been sent home, and I ate fruitcake in July that had been sealed in a can the previous November. That fruitcake had crossed the Atlantic three times, and there are not many fruitcakes that can make that statement. But I wasn't surprised, for I seem to have a gift for getting lost. Later, when I landed in New York, my service records said I was supposed to be in Berlin!

I first regretted the lost time, but then thought about the different experiences I had been a part of, and realized I wouldn't have gotten to see Sergeant DuPont's eyes pulsate after taking a belt of that tanning fluid, nor would I have been serenaded by the Polish Count lying on his back in the downpour.

When I thought of all the people that I had met in train depots, and in Austria, I was a little bit glad that the orders had gotten mixed up, because that sackful of memories would last a long time.

I was walking across the hospital grounds when I met the night nurse that had taken that guy from the 502nd and me off morphine. She seemed twice as pretty after I got to know her. She had a bag of compassion that she dragged around with one hand, counterbalanced by a bag of toughness she carried around with the other.

I said to her, "It's all over now and doesn't make any difference, but didn't you give me water that night you pulled us off morphine?"

This had been eight months earlier, but she quickly responded, "No, I gave the other guy water and gave you morphine."

I told her, "You got the needles mixed up!"

But she stuck to her guns and I didn't argue.

I was assigned to a ward in order to await my shipping orders. Most in this ward were mending limbs, and the person on ward duty was a German prisoner! He sat in a little room at the end of the ward and was not called upon to work unless someone needed help. He spoke fairly good English, and he had a great sense of humor, so we had some enjoyable conversations.

He told me how he had been captured. He was in a foxhole, and just as he peeped over the top of the hole, an artillery shell exploded very close. He dropped down in the hole and said to himself, "Surely those crazy Americans are not firing an artillery shell at one German soldier!" To check it out, he peeped over the top again and BOOM! — another shell hit in the same place. He dropped down in the hole and said to himself, "Yes, hell they are!"

He tied his handkerchief on the end of his rifle, stuck it up in the air, and waved it back and forth. Soon some American soldiers came and took him prisoner.

I learned some interesting things from him. When I first got to Germany, I had noticed that every pretty young woman would be pushing a baby buggy. I mentioned this to him, and he told me that these were the babies of the SS breeding program. The SS men were to take the finest and prettiest of young women and try to father as many children as possible in order to produce the best foundation for a "super race." Then, as the Hitler youth movement boys and girls got big enough, they would do the same. When the first generation got to child-bearing age, they could father and mother children within the ranks so that after a few generations there would be millions of young men and women that had been bred, born, and raised as elite SS troops, and these would be the leaders and governors of the lands that would be captured and resettled by Germans.

I gathered, from the German prisoner, that the regular Army men didn't particularly like the SS. If he saw a pretty girl on the street and proceeded to try to get acquainted, she could call the police if she didn't like it, and they would put him in jail. But, if an SS man approached a pretty girl on the street and she didn't like it and if she called the police, they would put her in jail.

This soldier's opinion was that Germany had paid one hell of a price for nothing.

Early in November of 1945, we were put on a train and sent to Cherbourg, France, where we were loaded onto a hospital ship — a converted Liberty ship — that took us home to the U.S. The crossing was pleasant and uneventful except for two days when we encountered a violent storm that caused the propeller to stay out of the water half of the time! The food was excellent, and I made a number of new friends. One in particular was a Sergeant from the 82nd Airborne Division that I came to know well. We had a lot in common and we would spend a good deal of time together while we were on the ship.

This soldier was very level-headed, had a great sense of humor about himself, and showed every indication that he was a dependable, easy-to-get-along with person. One thing was very obvious, though; he had a very pronounced stutter.

I didn't think he had this stutter when he was inducted into the Army, so I asked him what caused had it. I had assumed that it was due to a concussion, as a concussion had tangled my tongue as well. At any rate, soldiers have an easy way of discussing such things without being embarrassed, as some people might think. I was surprised when he chuckled and said, "I had a nervous breakdown."

I said, "Surely you don't mean that, because you don't act like a person who has nervous trouble." He didn't think so either, but that was what the medics said had happened.

"One night," he said, "I went to chow as on any other night. I didn't have a worry in the world; the war was over, and I would soon be going home. I had no problems. It just seemed like everything was right on target."

After chow he had started back to his barracks and when he was about halfway there, he was seized by a violent chill.

"I thought I was going to freeze to death before I could get to the medics. I could only think that I must be coming down with pneumonia or malaria or something like that."

But the medics never could find any sign of infection that would have caused this chill and they determined that he had had a nervous breakdown.

He laughed. "But you can't prove it by me, because I don't feel as if I had any kind of breakdown."

I asked him if he felt a little shaky or anything else in his thinking process that would indicate any problems and he said, "No, as far as I can tell, it has all just been physical."

The one thing that I did know was that the run-or-fight syndrome puts your body and nervous system on an entirely different level, and I suspected then and later from what happened to me that when the danger is finally over and the different systems of the body try to adjust back down, it's not always an even process.

Later on, I developed a tic that would cause my eye to wink. After the eye would wink, then a place somewhere else on my body would quiver, then another place, and so on. It began without reason and lasted about one month, and it stopped of its own accord. I just thought it was an adjustment taking place, a realignment of my self.

When we got home, it was like getting out of a jet and into an ox cart. Everyone seemed to react so slowly to situations that I couldn't see how they could have gotten anything accomplished.

After a year of light, semi-alert sleeping I began to sleep like a log, and everyone else seemed to speed back up to my usual ways. But I discovered

that I didn't like firecrackers anymore, especially if they were thrown
behind me.

Chapter Twenty

The Hospital and Home

*A*FTER WE FINALLY GOT OUT of that bad storm as we crossed the Atlantic for home, we sailed into New York harbor on smooth waters. An entertainment boat came out to meet us with a big dance band and a very pretty girl singing "Sentimental Journey." We unloaded on Staten Island and were taken across the bay to a hospital in New Jersey.

We had only been at the hospital a few days when we were loaded onto a train heading south. The Army had built and was operating a big hospital in Tuscaloosa, Alabama, for receiving military personnel and seeing to their treatment until they became well again, or were able to return to civilian life. I think every state had hospitals for this purpose, in order for the soldier to be close to his home while being treated. We got into Tuscaloosa in the middle of the night and when we unloaded, they took us to the hospital dining room where they served us a hot meal of liver smothered in onions. It was the best-prepared meal I had ever eaten, and I found out that this hospital had cooks who knew how to make ordinary food taste as if it was home-cooked.

There were two boys in the hospital from my home town, one with a broken leg and another with a hand shattered by a machine-gun bullet.

He told me that while he was under anesthetic, blowfly eggs had been put into his wound so that the maggots would eat the dead flesh and thus maybe the hand, such as it was, could be saved. But he was not told of this because no one can rest if he thinks maggots are aborning in his hand!

About two days later, as he was lying in bed he raised up his bandaged hand, and as he did so a fat maggot dropped out from under the bandage.

"Gawd amighty damn," he bellowed, "somebody come here quick, the flies done blowed me!"

As I looked around at the other patients in the hospital, seeing the terrible burn patients, and the wheelchair cases, and maybe more so the mental cases, I counted my blessings.

It was hard to imagine that there has ever been anyone in combat more scared than I, though of course, I have met a few who claimed they were! The truth is, though, that I knew a good many men that were broken not by fear, but by the horrible cold. In my case, as scared as I was, the brutal cold and unbearable conditions would rate ahead of fear as being the insurmountable circumstance that would have been my Waterloo. Knowing about the cold firsthand, I am also quite sure that the Marines in the Pacific Theater knew jungle rot, rain, heat, mosquitoes, and leeches more than they cared to.

Fear is not alone when it comes to breaking men; Mother Nature does a very good job when she puts her mind to it.

I had only been at this hospital a few days, when one morning they put our medical records on the foot of our beds. This meant we were about to have rounds. Soon a Captain came to me, and I removed my pajama top and he began the examination. At first he said, "I fail to see . . . " and then he said "Whoa! Colonel, would you please come over here?"

The Colonel in charge of orthopedics was young and very handsome sort of fellow. The Captain showed him my injury, and the Colonel put out his hand and touched me near the spine with his forefinger. After having examined me, he proceeded to tell the Captain all the things that I knew were in my medical record, which the Colonel had not seen. Then he elaborated and gave the prognosis. As he did this, I realized that I was in the presence of a very smart doctor. I put him in the same class as the Major who had treated me in France.

He told the Captain, "The Army doesn't need this man, and this man sure doesn't need the Army, so put him in for a medical discharge as of now."

Just as he finished, and the Captain was writing his instructions on a pad, a General and his clones walked up. This is when I found out that Generals like attention too.

The General said in a loud, expansive voice that could be heard all over the ward, "Colonel, has this soldier had his forty-five day furlough yet?" The Colonel began telling the General that he was in the process of discharging me from the Army, but the General was not hearing a word the Colonel said and interrupted him saying, "Colonel, I said has this man had his forty-five day furlough yet?"

This time the Colonel resignedly said, "No, Sir."

The General very emphatically told him to put me in for a furlough, "Immediately!"

The Colonel looked at me, arched his eyebrows slightly, barely shrugged his shoulders, and moved his head from side to side where only I could see his expression.

Soon I was dressed, and with furlough papers in hand, I was on a bus for home. I believe that a lot of soldiers coming home from a war feel a little self-conscious about going back into the midst of ordinary civilians. It seemed to me as if your experience has been so profound that you're somewhat like the odd man out. Too, there were a great many Gold Star mothers across the land and I could not help being aware of this.

Sometime after I left home the last time, before I went overseas, Mama, while repairing something in the house, fell off a stepladder and broke her leg. With that and complications from it she was bedfast for a long time. My sister at home had to work in the daytime and the only one to care for Mama during the day was her invalid sister. But Mama had graduated to crutches by this time, and things were looking up.

When I opened the front door, Mama was standing just to my left and as I stepped inside she reached over with her left hand and held her right crutch, came around with her right fist, and pretty near unjointed my shoulder and said, "Youuuuu devil, you!"

Index

by Lori L. Daniel